# A Dictionary
## of Latin Tags and Phrases

# A Dictionary
# of Latin Tags and
# Phrases

by
## EUGENE EHRLICH

ROBERT HALE · LONDON

© 1985, 1986 and 1987 Eugene Ehrlich
Introduction copyright © 1985 William F. Buckley, Jr.
First published in the United States of America as
*Amo, Amas, Amat and More*
First published in
Great Britain 1986 by arrangement with
Harper & Row Publishers, Inc., New York
as *Nil Desperandum*
This edition first published by arrangement with
Harper & Row Publishers, Inc., New York 1987

Reprinted 1989 (twice)
Reprinted 1991
Reprinted 1992

Robert Hale Limited
Clerkenwell House
Clerkenwell Green
London EC1R 0HT

British Library Cataloguing in Publication Data

Ehrlich, Eugene
   [Amo, amas, amat and more]. A dictionary
   of Latin tags and phrases.
   1. English language—Foreign words and
   phrases—Latin—Dictionaries   2. Latin
   language—Glossaries, vocabularies, etc.
   I. [Amo, amas, amat and more]   I. Title
   II. Ehrlich, Eugene. Nil Desperandum
   422'.471'03         PE1582.L3

ISBN 0-7090-3145-9

Photoset in North Wales by
Derek Doyle & Associates, Mold, Clwyd
Printed in Great Britain by
St Edmundsbury Press Ltd, Bury St Edmunds, Suffolk

# Contents

To
Emma and Dick

# Acknowledgements

I wish particularly to thank Christopher Dadian, of the Department of Classics, The Johns Hopkins University, who gave thoughtful attention to the translations. If any errors are still to be found in the work, they are my own responsibility. All that can be said at this time is *errare humanum est*, and while I would appreciate hearing from readers who find these errors, I would also hope to be forgiven.

My associates at The Hudson Group gave me support all through the joy of compiling this book. My long-time collaborator Gorton Carruth put up with my divided attention to other responsibilities. Hayden Carruth taught me the rudiments of the IBM Personal Computer so that an ancient language could be treated, perhaps for the first time ever, within the confines of a cathode ray tube. Only once did his ministrations fail to rescue me from the effects of my computer illiteracy: at one time I lost an entire section of the book somewhere within the computer memory, and for all I know, it is lurking there to this day. Raymond Hand, Jr., helped free me for work on this book and assisted with the free renderings of certain Latin proverbs.

The above-mentioned personal computer obviates acknowledgement of a typist's help, but a final word must be added for the help in indexing supplied by Felice Levy, who has participated with me on many editorial projects.

# Preface

The idea for this book came quickly, as do most of my ideas for books. The execution was not as fast. Years of collecting expressions suitable for inclusion, followed by months of translation and writing, have finally yielded a volume I hope will prove entertaining as well as instructive for readers.

A word must be said about the choice of expressions. Utility was the principal criterion. There is no doubt that readers are plagued by writers and speakers who blithely drop Latin phrases into their English sentences with no hint of translation. Without questioning the motives of the Latin-droppers, one can safely say that most modern audiences require some assistance. Word-for-word translations provided in some English dictionaries do not always suffice, so the attempt is made in many entries of this book to supply more enlightening free translations as well as literal translations. Besides helping readers and listeners to cope with Latin used by others, it is hoped that using this book will spare its readers the ignominy of an infelicitous choice when they venture into Latin. The most common misuse I encounter is the confusion of 'e.g.' with 'i.e.', but there are many others. Once 'e.g.' and 'i.e.' were accepted for inclusion in this book, it became necessary to treat in the list of entries all but the most arcane scholarly abbreviations and expressions.

Medical and pharmacological Latin were never serious candidates for inclusion: prescriptions are filled a million or more times a day without the Latin once required to say 'take twice a day' and the like. But Latin is still seen in everyday writing about matters of law, and the law is a serious matter. The problem was to limit the number of entries of this type to those most frequently encountered – consider *in re* and *corpus delicti* and a multitude of others. Fortunately, engineers, computer scientists, electronics experts and other modern wizards hit their stride long after Latin

9

had disappeared from most school curricula, so they make no contribution to this volume despite the fact that modern Latin words are continually being devised to enable the Vatican to deal knowledgeably with modern science and technology, just as modern Hebrew must face this requirement. Of course, it is not only ancient languages that must cope with this problem. Modern English, in fact, brings new words into use every day, sometimes inventing them – often from Latin and Greek sources – and sometimes adding meanings to existing English words. Indeed, where appropriate, English accomplishes its purpose by borrowing existing words from modern foreign languages.

While the majority of the entries in this book date back to classical times, there is some treatment of phrases that came into use during the Middle Ages. As will be seen, some of the Latin included in the entry list is used – should one say was used? – in church services.

Once the list of candidate entries had grown to reflect these many sources and areas of learning, a much more difficult task had to be accomplished, that of selecting, among a vast number of available maxims and proverbs, those that would be most interesting and useful for the modern reader. One principle of selection was the inherent wisdom reflected in the thought. Another was the insight into a civilization implicit in a thought. As I worked through the entry list again and again, I was struck by the universality of people's problems throughout the ages, and the satisfying solutions afforded, despite the often contradictory nature of these solutions. It is hoped that the reader will share the pleasure of this recognition.

So this book took shape, sometimes growing recklessly and demanding to be pruned, at other times crying out for fuller treatment of a particular topic.

EUGENE EHRLICH

# Introduction

*by William F. Buckley, Jr.*

It is not plain to me why I was asked to write the introduction to this book. (There are true Latinists around. Not in abundance, but for instance one thinks of Garry Wills and Ernest van den Haag, just to mention two noisy, and brilliant, writers.) Nor is it obvious why I accepted the invitation (the little stipend is being forwarded to charity).

I suppose I am asked because the few Latin phrases I am comfortable with I tend to use without apology. For instance, for some reason I find it handier even in idiomatic exchanges to say *'per impossibile'* over against, say, 'assuming that the impossible were actually to take place'. Nor is the usefulness of *per impossibile sui generis* – if you see the kind of situation one is capable of falling into.

So, there are those Latin phrases – and, really, there are not so many of them – that cling to life because they seem to perform useful duties without any challenger rising up to take their place in English. Sometimes these special exemptions from vernaculariz-ation in the mother tongue derive from the distinctive inflection that flows in from the Latin. There is no English substitute, really, for 'He faced the problem *ad hoc,*' which is much easier than the cumbersome alternative in English ('He faced the problem with exclusive concern given to the circumstances that particularly surrounded it'). Other Latin phrases, the kind against which Fowler inveighed, have the sense of being dragged in, and the reader, when he comes across them, will judge on the basis of circumstances whether he is on to a felicitous intonation communicated by the Latin and not by the English. The scholarly Mr Ehrlich, for instance, includes in this collection *'Ab asino lanam',* giving as the English meaning (which is different from the

11

English translation), 'blood from a stone'. And further elucidating, 'Anyone who tries to achieve the impossible is doomed to failure. Thus, an attempt to get *ab asino lanam*, literally, "wool from an ass", will inevitably fail.' The above is for the scholar, not the practitioner of idiom.

But then why not? Mr Ehrlich, in his introduction, touches on the difficulty of assembling a list meagrely. Inevitably some readers would be dissatisfied. For all one knows, there is someone about who day in and day out denounces efforts to reason with the Soviets as ventures *ab asino lanam*, and it would ruin their life if a collection of Latin sayings were published that left out that expression. Better, then, to include '*ab asino lanam*', and the kitchen sink; which Mr Ehrlich does, and I am very glad that he decided to do so.

Probably the principal Latin-killer this side of the Huns was Vatican II. The other day, sitting alongside a Jesuit college president, I mentioned, by way of indicating the distinctive training of English Jesuits, that my schoolmasters at Beaumont College, when engaged in faculty discussions, addressed each other in Latin. He replied matter-of-factly that so it had been with him and his classmates. 'But now, after fifteen years, I would have a problem with relatively simple Latin.'

No doubt about it, the generations of Catholic priests trained in Latin, and the seepage of Latin to parishioners, students and altar boys, will diminish, drying up the spring which for so many centuries watered the general knowledge of Latin, and held out almost exclusively, after the virtual desertion of Latin from curricula in which it held, in e.g. British public schools, an absolutely patriarchal position. But it is not likely that the remaining bits and pieces will all be extirpated by the vernacular juggernaut. And even if that were so, it would happen generations down the line. Meanwhile I know of no book to contend in usefulness with that of Mr Ehrlich, who has given us this resourceful, voluminous and appetizing *smorgasbord*.

# Dramatis Personae

Caesar. *Gaius Iulius Caesar.* 100–44 BC. Born at Rome. Soldier, statesman. *Bellum Gallicum (The Gallic War)*, *Bellum civile (The Civil War)*.

Cato. *Marcus Porcius Cato.* 241–149 BC. Born in Tusculum in central Italy. Roman statesman. *De agricultura (On Agriculture)*.

Catullus. *Gaius Valerius Catullus.* 84?–54? BC. Born at Verona in Cisalpine Gaul. Best known for his tempestuous love affair with a Roman gentlewoman (probably the notorious Clodia), whom he immortalized in his poems under the pseudonym Lesbia. *Carmina (Poems)*.

Cicero. *Marcus Tullius Cicero.* 106–43 BC. Born at Arpinum in central Italy. Jurist, statesman, writer, philosopher. *Orationes (Orations)*, *Rhetorica (Writings on Rhetoric)*, *Philosophica (Political and Philosophical Writings)*, *Epistulae (Letters)*.

Claudian. *Claudius Claudianus.* AD 4th century–*c.* 404. From Alexandria. A speaker of Greek. Came to Italy and mastered Latin, which was the language of his writings. Court poet under the Emperor Honorius; his poetry eulogized his patrons. *De consulatu Honorii (On the Consulship of Honorius)*, *De consulatu Stilichonis (On the Consulship of Stilicho)*.

Epicurus. 341–270 BC. Born on Samos, a Greek island in the Aegean. Moral and natural philosopher. Our knowledge of his system derives to a great extent from the Roman poet Lucretius. *Epistulae (Letters)*, Κύριαι Δοξαι *(Kyriai Doxai, Principal Doctrines)*.

Horace. *Quintus Horatius Flaccus.* 65–8 BC. Born at Venusia in southern Italy. Member of the literary circle brought together by Maecenas under the patronage of the Emperor Augustus. *Carmina (Odes)*, *Epodi (Epodes)*, *Satirae (Satires)*, *Epistulae (Verse Letters)*, *Ars Poetica (The Poetic Art)*.

Juvenal. *Decimus Iunius Iuvenalis.* AD 1st–2nd century. Born at Aquinum, Italy. Author of verse satires attacking corruption of Roman society. *Satirae (Satires).*

Livy. *Titus Livius.* 59 BC–AD 17 or 64 BC–AD 12. Born at Padua in north-eastern Italy. Historian. *Ab urbe condita* ([History of Rome] *from the Founding of the City).*

Lucan. *Marcus Annaeus Lucanus.* AD 39–65. Born at Córdoba in Spain. Courtier in the reign of Nero. Fell from grace and eventually was forced to commit suicide after becoming implicated in the Pisonian conspiracy. *Pharsalia.*

Lucretius. *Titus Lucretius Carus.* Probably 94–55 BC. Probably member of an aristocratic Roman family, the Lucretii. Poet and philosopher. *De rerum natura (On the Nature of the Universe).*

Manilius. *Marcus Manilius.* 1st century BC–AD 1st century. Facts of his life unknown. *Astronomica* (a didactic poem on astrology).

Marcus Aurelius. *Marcus Aurelius Antoninus.* AD 161–180. Roman emperor. *Meditationes (Meditations).*

Martial. *Marcus Valerius Martialus. c.* AD 40–*c.* 104. Born at Bilbilis in Spain. Depicted Roman society in epigrammatic verse. *Epigrammata (Epigrams).*

Ovid. *Publius Ovidius Naso.* 43 BC–AD 17. Born at Sulmo in central Italy. Intended by his father for a legal career but gave it up to devote himself to poetry. Member of the literary circle of Messalla. Exiled to an island in the Black Sea by Augustus, who was offended by Ovid's *Ars Amatoria,* though there may have been other offences as well. *Amores (Love Poems), Ars Amatoria (The Amatory Art), Metamorphoses.*

Persius. *Aulus Persius Flaccus.* AD 34–62. Born at Volaterrae in northern Italy. Stoic satirist. *Satirae (Satires).*

Petronius. *Petronius Arbiter.* AD 1st century. Probably the courtier referred to by Tacitus as Nero's *arbiter elegantiae. Satyricon.*

Phaedrus. *c.* 15 BC–*c.* AD 50. A Thracian born a slave. Eventually became freedman in the household of the Emperor Augustus. *Fabulae (Fables).*

Plautus. *Titus Maccius Plautus.* 3rd–2nd centuries BC. Born at Sarsina in central Italy. Author of comic dramas based on Greek originals.

Pliny the Elder. *Gaius Plinius.* AD 23/4–79. Born at Comum, now Como, in north central Italy. Military commander in Germany, provincial administrator, counsellor to Emperors Vespasian and

Titus. *Naturalis historia (Natural History).*

Pliny the Younger. *Gaius Plinius Caecilius Secundus. c.* AD 66–*c.* 112. Nephew and adopted son of Pliny the Elder. Senatorial career; lawyer, civil administrator. *Epistulae (Letters).*

Plutarch. L. (?) *Mestrius Plutarchus.* Before AD 50–after 120. Born and lived most of his life in Chaeronea, in north-eastern Greece. Prolific (over two hundred titles attributed to him) and influential. *Moralia, Vitae (Lives).*

Publilius Syrus. 1st century BC. Came to Rome as a slave, perhaps from Antioch. Author of mimes. *Sententiae (Maxims).*

Quintilian. *Marcus Fabius Quintilianus. c.* AD 30–before 100. Born at Calagurris in Spain. Teacher of rhetoric; among his pupils was Pliny the Younger. *Institutio oratoria (The Teaching of Oratory).*

Seneca the Elder. *Lucius Annaeus Seneca. c.* 55 BC–between AD 37 and 41. Born at Córdoba in Spain. Student of and writer on rhetoric. *Controversiae, Suasoriae.*

Seneca the Younger. *Lucius Annaeus Seneca.* Between 4 and 1 BC–AD 65. Born at Córdoba in Spain. Son of Seneca the Elder, counsellor to Nero, philosopher, poet. *Dialogi (Dialogues), Naturales quaestiones (Natural Questions,* enquiries in physical science, *Apocolocyntosis (The Pumpkinification* [of the Emperor Claudius]), *Tragedies, Epigrams.*

Suetonius. *Gaius Suetonius Tranquillus. c.* AD 69–? Practised law briefly, held various posts in the imperial service, secretary to the Emperor Hadrian. *De vita Caesarum (Lives of the Caesars* [from Julius to Domitian]).

Tacitus. *Cornelius Tacitus. c.* 56 AD–after 115. Probably from northern Italy or Gaul. Historian, held several official posts. *Annales (Annals), Historiae (Histories), Agricola* ([biography of his father-in-law, Cneius Iulius] *Agricola), Germania.*

Terence. *Publius Terentius Afer. c.* 190–159 BC. Born in North Africa, brought to Rome as a slave. Author of comic dramas adapted from Greek models by Apollodorus of Carystus and Menander. *Andria (The Girl from Andros), Hecyra (The Mother-in-Law), Heauton timorumenos (The Self-Punisher), Eunuchus (The Eunuch), Phormio, Adelphi (The Brothers).*

Tertullian. *Quintus Septimius Florens Tertullianus. c.* AD 160–*c.* 240. Born at Carthage in North Africa. Trained as a lawyer. Converted to Christianity at the age of thirty-five, wrote in defence of his new faith and on moral, ethical and religious problems.

Varro. *Marcus Terentius Varro.* 116–27 BC. Born at Reate in central Italy. Wrote on language, education, history, biography, philosophy, music, medicine, architecture, literary history and philology. *De lingua latina (On the Latin Language).*

Vegetius. *Flavius Vegetius Renatus.* AD 4th–5th century. Bureaucrat in the imperial service. *Epitome rei militaris (Manual of Military Affairs).*

Virgil. *Publius Vergilius Maro.* 70–19 BC. Born near Mantua in north-eastern Italy. Early in his career deeply influenced by Catullus, member of the literary circle of Asinius Pollio. Later, through Maecenas, came under the patronage of the Emperor Augustus. *Aeneid, Georgics, Eclogues.*

## ab absurdo
from the absurd

One who argues *ab absurdo* seeks to establish the validity of his position by pointing out the absurdity of his opponent's position. While an argument *ab absurdo* may have the effect of demolishing one's opponent's position in debate, it usually does not of itself prove the validity of one's own position.

## ab aeterno
since the beginning of time

Anything that has existed *ab aeterno*, literally 'from eternity', has no assignable date of origin. This phrase can be used to describe almost any human folly: 'Wars have been fought *ab aeterno*.'

## ab asino lanam
blood from a stone

Anyone who tries to achieve the impossible is doomed to failure. Thus, an attempt to get *ab asino lanam*, literally 'wool from an ass', will inevitably fail.

## ab extra
from the outside

This phrase, the opposite of *ab intra*, finds use in such thoughts as 'We are mistaken in believing that peace will come to the Middle East through the efforts *ab extra* of world powers.'

**ab imo pectore**
from the heart

When we speak from the heart, we speak sincerely, but the Romans spoke *ab imo pectore*, literally 'from the bottom of the breast (or chest)'.

**ab incunabulis**
from infancy

The Latin word *incunabula* may be translated as 'cradle, swaddling clothes, infancy, or origin'. The English 'incunabula' refers to the earliest stage or beginning of anything but most often to copies of books that date back to the period before AD 1500, when the use of movable type in printing was in its formative stage. The Latin *ab incunabulis* has nothing to do with books.

**ab initio**
from the beginning

The Latin equivalent of 'from the start' or 'from inception'. 'Lack of adequate capital doomed the company to failure *ab initio*.' (See *ab origine* and *ab ovo*.)

**ab intra**
from within

The insider's role is played out *ab intra*. 'The only hope for reform of an institution is through effort expended *ab intra*.'

**ab irato**
unfair, unprovoked

This phrase may be taken literally as 'from an angry man'. Thus, any action taken *ab irato* is to be understood as arising from anger rather than reason, and responses to such actions will be weighed carefully by reasonable people. 'The attack was *ab irato*: the victim had no chance to defend himself.'

**ab origine**
from the first

*Ab origine* may be translated as 'from the very beginning, source, or origin'. The English word 'aborigine' – the preferred form is aboriginal' – comes directly from this phrase and means 'original or earliest known inhabitant of a place'. 'Scholars who are interested in gaining full understanding of an institution, for example, find it valuable to pursue *ab origine* studies in the hope that knowledge of the beginnings of an institution under study will shed light on its present status.' (See *ab initio* and *ab ovo*.)

## ab ovo
from the very beginning

The literal meaning of *ab ovo* is 'from the egg', so a thorough search is a search *ab ovo*, a thorough analysis is an analysis *ab ovo*, and a complete presentation is one made *ab ovo*. It is interesting to note, however, that *ab ovo* may imply a tedious thoroughness: 'Once again we were subjected to a sententious *ab ovo* account that lasted more than an hour and lulled most of us to sleep.' (See *ab initio* and *ab origine*.)

## ab ovo usque ad mala
from start to finish

A colourful Roman phrase reminiscent of our own 'from soup to nuts', since it is literally translated as 'from the egg to the apples' but with a meaning that is quite different. 'From soup to nuts' refers to completeness – for example, of a multi-course dinner or a salesman's catalogue. *Ab ovo usque ad mala*, by contrast, means 'from start to finish'. The expression derives from the fact that Roman dinners often began with eggs and ended with fruit. 'Your plan was inadequate *ab ovo usque ad mala* and had no chance for success.'

## absit invidia
no offence intended

When we say *absit invidia*, literally 'let ill will be absent', our words reflect the power that Romans attributed to animosity, whether or not openly expressed. They believed, as do many people today, that ill feelings toward someone could cause that person great harm, so they absolved themselves of the intention to harm someone by saying *absit invidia* – the English expressions 'no offence' and 'no offence intended', by comparison, are mere social gestures intended to prevent ill feelings. *Absit invidia* may also be extended: **absit invidia verbo** means 'May it be said without giving offence'. (See *absit omen*.)

## absit omen
may this not be an omen

The rough equivalent of 'Protect me, O Lord', *absit omen*, literally 'May the omen be absent', was used to invoke divine protection against evil when something foreboding occurred. The Romans, strong believers in divination, employed soothsayers to interpret omens as a means of foretelling the future. Soothsayers were so popular that the Romans had many words for these practitioners, among them *auspex* and *haruspex*. An *auspex* relied on observation of the behaviour of birds to foretell the future, and we are indebted to this highly specialized word for our own words 'auspices' and 'auspicious'. A *haruspex* found special value in examining the entrails of sacrificial animals to foretell the future but also made interpretations based on less gory activities, such as observation of lightning and other natural phenomena. While we do not pay as much attention to omens today, there are those who may say *absit omen* or its equivalent – 'knock on wood'? – when a black cat crosses in front of them.

## ab uno disce omnes
from one example learn about all

This maxim, literally 'from one learn all', found in Virgil's *Aeneid*, applies to situations in which the import of a single observation is universally applicable. It is careless application of *ab uno disce omnes* that may trap us in faulty generalizations.

## ab urbe condita
since the founding of the city

Abbreviated AUC. The city referred to is ancient Rome, *the* city of its day. Romans dated years from the founding of their city, in 753 BC. Tradition has it that in that year Romulus and his twin brother, Remus, built Rome. In infancy the twins were thrown into the Tiber, the river still running through modern Rome, but were saved by a shepherd and suckled by a wolf. Romulus became the first king of Rome upon its founding. Remus was put to death because he mocked his brother's city. *Ab urbe condita* is also given as *anno urbis conditae*, 'in the year of the founding of the city', also abbreviated AUC.

## abusus non tollit usum
misuse does not nullify proper use

Broadly applied, the maxim teaches that the value of a procedure, an object etc. is not destroyed by improper use. The helicopter, for example, was thought of by its principal inventor as a life-saving machine. If *abusus non tollit usum* is correct, the machine's use in war does not mean the helicopter itself is evil. The value of television as an instructional medium, to take another example, is not destroyed by those who watch it all day long. In yet another sense, the maxim may be applied by prescriptive linguists to what they construe as corruptions in usage. *Abusus non tollit usum* for them means that improper use of a word does not destroy its proper use, and those who deal imprecisely with the language are not given *carte blanche* to work their destructive ways. Recognizing the Latin maxim, Eric Partridge entitled one of his works on language *Usage and Abusage*. There is another form of *abusus non tollit usum*, which is recognized by jurists as conveying that same thought: **ab abusu ad usum non valet consequentia**, 'The consequences of abuse do not apply to general use', suggesting that a right should not be withheld because some people abuse it.

## abyssus abyssum invocat
one false step leads to another

A warning, literally 'hell calls hell', in the Psalms of David and a typically Roman maxim as well. In *The Screwtape Letters*, C.S. Lewis said: 'The safest road to Hell is the gradual one – the gentle slope, soft underfoot, without sudden turnings, without milestones, without signposts.' We can easily see that the first cigarette, the first drink of whisky, the first step down any inviting path, is difficult to prevent, yet we must always be on guard: *Abyssus abyssum invocat.*

## a capite ad calcem
thoroughly

Literally 'from head to heel', *a capite ad calcem* may be thought of as the Latin equivalent of 'from top to bottom' or 'from stem to stern'. 'The candidate, claiming that the entire municipal government was rotten, promised a reorganization *a capite ad calcem.*'

## accessit
honourable mention

This word literally means 'he (or she) came near', but in academic settings, particularly in European universities, an *accessit* is the recognition awarded the runner-up in a competition for a medal or other honour. Academic terminology still relies to a great extent on Latin. This is not surprising, since the earliest universities were concerned primarily with, and conducted their official business in, classical languages. *Accessit* has a certain cachet: 'I had hoped to win first prize, but I knew I would be content with an *accessit*' is far more comforting than 'honourable mention'.

## Acheruntis pabulum
food for the gallows

*Acheruntis pabulum* should not be applied willy-nilly to all the poor wretches who sit on death row, but only to those who may be thought of as deserving to die. Acheron – the Romans called it *Acheruns* – was one of seven rivers said to flow around Hell. Thus, any person adjudged sufficiently evil may be said to be *Acheruntis pabulum*, literally 'food of Acheron'.

## a cruce salus
salvation (comes) from the cross

The cross is, of course, the symbol of the death of Christ, and Christ's death meant redemption for His followers. Thus, *a cruce salus* is the teaching that salvation comes from belief in Christianity.

## acta est fabula
it's all over

In the classical theatre, with no curtain to draw across the stage, the words *acta est fabula*, literally 'The drama has been acted out', signified the end of a performance. In another context, Emperor Augustus is said to have uttered *'Acta est fabula'* just before he died, establishing a pattern followed by Rabelais, whose last words are said to have been *'La farce est jouée'*, 'The farce is ended'. *Acta est fabula* may be spoken appropriately whenever a life or an unfolding event comes to an unhappy end, or one could say, 'It's curtains.'

## acta sanctorum
deeds of the saints

Accounts of the lives of the Christian martyrs and saints are used in teaching the faith. The most famous collection is the monumental *Acta Sanctorum*, initiated by the Bollandists, a group named for Jean Bolland, a seventeenth-century Flemish Jesuit, and in English usually called *Lives of the Saints*. This great work, still the responsibility of the Bollandists, is arranged according to the dates of the ecclesiastical calendar. It is approaching seventy volumes in length and still growing.

## ad absurdum
to absurdity

See *reductio ad absurdum*.

## ad arbitrium
at pleasure

Anything done of one's own will is performed *ad arbitrium*. 'In this life, how many actions are really taken *ad arbitrium*?' Another expression, for the same thought is **arbitrio suo**, 'on his (or her) own authority'.

## ad astra per aspera
to the stars through difficulties

We achieve great things only by encountering and overcoming adversity.

**ad augusta per angusta**
to honours through difficulties

*Augusta* refers to holy places, *angusta* to narrow spaces. This maxim tells us, therefore, that we cannot achieve great results without suffering, the suffering being represented here by squeezing through narrow spaces. A fit motto for dieters.

**ad calendas graecas**
never

The literal translation of this Roman version of 'when hell freezes over' is 'at the Greek calends'. The rub is that the calends, the first day of the month, was a feature of the Roman calendar, and the Greeks had no calends. It was on the calends that interest on borrowed money was to be paid, so for Roman debtors they were *tristes calendae*, 'the unhappy calends'.

**ad captandum vulgus**
in order to win over the masses

Actions taken *ad captandum vulgus* are intended to please the common people. The implication is that such actions may not be in the best interest of society but are intended only to achieve popularity. Politicians campaigning for office, for example, are wont to promise reforms *ad captandum vulgus* and never give a thought to accomplishing them.

**ad clerum**
to the clergy

A statement made by a Church leader and intended only for the ears of the clergy is made *ad clerum*, as opposed to a statement *ad populum*, 'to the people'.

**a Deo et Rege**
from God and the King

Divine monarchs saw themselves as representatives of God on earth, so documents issued by them were often signed *a Deo et Rege*.

**adeste fideles**
O come, all ye faithful

A Christmas hymn written in Latin, date and author uncertain.

**ad eundem gradum**
to the same degree

Often abbreviated *ad eundem*, this phrase can be used to apportion blame or praise justly among parties to a deed. 'The judge held both litigants accountable *ad eundem*.' *Ad eundem gradum* has a special use when applied to academic life. Construing *gradum* as an academic rank, under special circumstances a student holding a Master of Arts degree from one university may be awarded the same degree by another university without examination, such degree being termed 'MA *ad eundem gradum*'.

**ad gloriam**
for glory

See *ad maiorem Dei Gloriam*.

**ad gustum**
to one's taste

A cookery book expression. 'Add salt *ad gustum*.'

**ad hoc**
for this (purpose)

An *ad hoc* committee is a temporary committee established to accomplish a particular task. Once an *ad hoc* committee has completed the job for which it was established, it is disbanded.

**ad hominem**
against the man

See *ad rem* and *argumentum ad hominem*.

**adhuc sub iudice** (or **judice) lis est**
the case is still before the court

Members of the legal profession are enjoined from public discussion of any matters that are under adjudication (*sub iudice*).

People under indictment and public officials accused of misconduct in office may invoke *adhuc sub iudice lis est* as a means of avoiding public discussion of their problems.

## ad infinitum
without limit

Abbreviated **ad inf.** and **ad infin.**, this phrase is the Latin equivalent of 'forever, to infinity, endlessly'. 'Her husband went on *ad infinitum* on the question of equal division of household chores.' (See *ad nauseam*.)

## ad interim
in the meantime

This phrase, which has an English counterpart, 'in the interim', is often abbreviated **ad int.**

## ad kalendas graecas
never

Alternative spelling for *ad calendas graecas*.

## ad libitum
extemporaneously

Literally meaning 'at pleasure' and abbreviated **ad lib.** in Latin, this expression is popularly used as a noun phrase or modifier in English in the form 'ad lib' to express absence of planning. 'His worst jokes were carefully planned ad libs.'

## ad limina apostolorum
to the highest authority

This expression, literally 'to the thresholds of the Apostles', is applied to matters appropriate for papal consideration and disposition before the tombs of St Peter and St Paul. Often abbreviated *ad limina*, the expression finds its widest use in more mundane applications: 'The chairman of the Romance Languages Department suggested that the committee was beyond its authority and that the matter be taken *ad limina*.' In such a case, the question would surely be settled by higher university authority.

## ad litem
for the suit or action

Among lawyers, an *ad litem* decision is taken as valid only for the *lis*, the controversy under adjudication. Thus, a guardian *ad litem* is appointed by a court to act for a minor only in regard to the problem of the minor before the court, not to serve as a substitute father.

## ad litteram (also literam)
to the last jot

*Littera* has as one of its meanings 'letter of the alphabet'. *Ad litteram*, literally 'to the letter', means 'precisely'. 'We must live up to our agreement *ad litteram*.'

## ad locum
at or to the place

Abbreviated **ad loc**.

## ad maiorem Dei gloriam
for the greater glory of God

Motto of the Society of Jesuits. The abbreviation AMDG appears as an epigraph in books produced by the Jesuit order. The full expression is sometimes cited as the rationale for actions taken by any Christians.

## ad nauseam
to the point of (causing) nausea

Anything unpleasurable that appears to go on endlessly may be said to be proceeding *ad nauseam*, literally 'to seasickness'. The clear meaning of this phrase is that such activity has reached the point at which it is almost more than a body can bear. Nothing that gives pleasure can properly be described in this way. 'The lecturer went on *ad nauseam*, apparently determined to read to us every last word in his notes.'

**ad patres**
dead

The literal translation of *ad patres* is 'to the fathers' or 'to the ancestors'. To go *ad patres* is to die; to send someone *ad patres* is to kill that person.

**ad perpetuam rei memoriam**
for the perpetual remembrance of the thing

Words traditionally used to open papal bulls.

**ad populum**
to the people

*Populus* means 'the entire people'. An *ad populum* statement is one intended for the ears of the masses.

**ad praesens ova cras pullis sunt meliora**
a bird in the hand is worth two in the bush

This conservative maxim translates literally as 'Eggs today are better than chickens tomorrow'. The advice is appropriate for all who take risks, e.g., stockbrokers' clients. It is usually more prudent to hold on to what one has than to risk everything in speculation.

**ad quem**
for (or to) which (or whom)

**ad referendum**
for further consideration

*Ad referendum*, which translates literally as 'for referring', is a diplomats' term. Diplomats who accept a proposal *ad referendum* indicate by their actions that final acceptance is dependent on the approval of their governments. *Referendum* has come over directly into English with the meaning of 'a vote by all qualified voters on a matter of public concern'.

**ad rem**
to the matter at hand

*Ad rem*, literally 'to the thing', can be rendered in various ways. With the meaning 'pertinent' or 'relevant': 'The barrister was admonished to make only *ad rem* comments or be silent.' 'In a straightforward manner': 'Because of the limitation on debate, it is vital to speak *ad rem* if we are to conclude our considerations within the allotted time.' Above all, it must be noted that *ad rem* is the phrase that contrasts with *ad hominem*. Debaters who argue *ad rem* address the matter at hand to score points in the debate; debaters who argue *ad hominem* attack their opponents to score points.

**adsum**
present!

A formal answer to a roll-call, literally 'I am here'.

**ad unguem**
perfectly

This phrase, literally 'to a fingernail', is used to convey the thought of accomplishing something well or precisely. A sculptor in ancient times would test the smoothness of a finished surface by running a fingernail over it.

**ad unum omnes**
unanimously

Literally 'all to one'. 'The delegates accepted the resolution *ad unum omnes*.'

**ad usum Delphini**
expurgated

A modern Latin phrase, translated literally as 'for the Dauphin's use'. An edition of classic works prepared for the Dauphin, heir to the throne of Louis XIV of France, carried the title *Ad usum Delphini*. The works, as might be expected, were expurgated to avoid offending the young man, so any expurgated work today may be termed *ad usum Delphini*.

**ad utrumque paratus**
prepared for the worst

A mature person is ready to cope with any eventuality, including the final one. The Romans described such a person as *ad utrumque paratus*, literally 'ready for either (eventuality)'. (See *semper paratus*.)

**ad valorem**
in proportion to value

Abbreviated **ad val**. An import duty fixed *ad valorem* is one established on the basis of the commercial value of the imported item. Like death and taxes, *ad valorem* has been with us so long that it now is part of the English language.

**ad verbum**
verbatim

The phrase *ad verbum*, literally 'to the word', is the Roman equivalent of the English 'verbatim', which is a direct borrowing from medieval Latin. (See *verbatim et litteratim*.) The Romans had several other expressions for 'word-for-word': **e verbo, de verbo,** and **pro verbo**. Perhaps this tells us something about the difficulty of making accurate copies before printing was invented.

**adversa**
things noted

A scholarly expression referring to observations one has made.

**adversaria**
a journal

*Adversaria*, literally 'that which has been turned to', is a plural noun referring to notes or brief written comments. 'Her *adversaria* were fascinating in their perceptions.' It also refers to annotations or commentaries written on a facing page of a book. As a singular noun, an *adversaria* is a journal or commonplace book, a book used for recording one's observations as well as for collecting poems, brief essays and any other material one finds worth keeping.

**adversus solem ne loquitor**
don't waste your time arguing the obvious

This maxim advises one literally, 'Don't speak against the sun'. When confronted by an all-important, irrefutable fact, there is no point in disputing further. The smoking gun, the tell-tale blond hair, the lipstick smudge, all signal the end of the discussion for any reasonable culprit: it is time for plea bargaining. (See *in flagrante delicto*.)

**ad vitam**
for life

A legal term sometimes found in wills, with the meaning of 'for use during a person's life only'. (See *ad vitam aut culpam*.)

**ad vitam aeternam**
forever

*Ad vitam aeternam*, literally 'for eternal life', conveys the idea of 'for all time'. 'Here is the money, but know that this is payment *ad vitam aeternam*.'

**ad vitam aut culpam**
for life or until a misdeed

The origin of *ad vitam aut culpam* rests in the feudal practice of conveying property or privilege that would not revert to the grantor until the death or misbehaviour of the person receiving the benefit. One can see that such a grant might impose discipline on the recipient to behave properly or risk loss of the beneficence. Today, any gift given with strings attached, such as a car to one's son on condition that he drive it safely, might be said to be made *ad vitam aut culpam*.

**advocatus diaboli**
devil's advocate

The Roman Catholic Church uses the term *promotor fidei*, 'promoter of the faith', or *advocatus diaboli*, to designate the Church official appointed to argue against a proposed canonization or beatification. It is this official's responsibility to find the flaws in the evidence presented by those who support the proposed designation of the *beatus*, 'the blessed person'. In this trial of opposing forces, it is expected that the truth will emerge to support or deny canonization. A person playing devil's advocate today is too often a person fond of taking the unpopular side of any issue under discussion, and primarily for the sake of argument.

### aeger
sick

In Latin, *aeger* as a noun means 'an invalid'; as an adjective it means 'sick'. In British universities, *aeger* is the traditional term used on students' medical excuses for failing to appear for an examination, and a medical excuse itself may also be called an *aeger*. (See *aegrotat*.)

### aegrescit medendo
the remedy is worse than the disease

*Aegrescit medendo*, Virgil's phrase, literally means 'The disease worsens with the treatment'. Those who question the efficacy of some medical treatment may use this phrase appropriately as their battlecry.

### aegri somnia
a sick man's dreams

An *aegri somnia*, Horace's phrase, may be translated more freely as 'a hallucination'. 'They tend to treat everything I say as an *aegri somnia*.' The Romans appear to have been acutely aware of the role of the emotions in causing symptoms of illness. Virgil spoke of **aegra amans**, 'lover's disease', and Livy spoke of **aeger amore** to describe the same condition, in apt recognition of the pathology of romance.

### aegrotat
a note from the doctor

*Aegrotat* literally means 'He (or she) is sick'. Thus, in British universities, an *aegrotat* is an official medical excuse. (See *aeger*.) But the meaning extends beyond that. An *aegrotat* is also an unclassified degree that may be granted by a British university to a student who completes all academic requirements save final examinations, if the student is too sick to sit for the examinations.

### aequam servare mentem
to keep one's cool

*Aequam servare mentem*, which translates literally as 'to keep an unruffled mind', recognizes the value of maintaining a clear head while conducting the business of life, especially when making important decisions. Horace, in his *Odes*, suggested **aequam memento rebus in arduis servare mentem**, adjuring us to remember to maintain a clear head when attempting difficult tasks.

### aequo animo
calmly

*Aequo animo*, literally 'with a calm mind', refers to evenness of mental attitude. Anyone who has composure or equanimity usually behaves *aequo animo*.

### aere perennius
everlasting

The Romans who knew the characteristics of certain metals, used the word *aes* for copper and its alloys, brass and bronze. When, therefore, they wished to respond to someone who had done a favour, they might use *aere perennius*, literally 'more durable than bronze', to suggest that the friendship shown would last forever. Certainly a more felicitous response than 'I owe you one.'

### aetatis suae
of his (or her) age

*Aetatis* alone means 'of the age', while *aetatis suae* means 'in a particular year of one's life'. Tombstones once carried such inscriptions as 'Died *aetatis suae* 37', or 'AS 37'. *Aetatis suae* is also given as **anno aetatis suae**, meaning 'in the year of his (or her) age'.

**aeternum vale**
farewell forever

A suitable inscription for a tombstone, perhaps also a suitable phrase to use when ending a love affair.


**a fortiori**
with stronger reason

*A fortiori* can be interpreted as meaning 'even more certain' or 'all the more'. Thus we can say: 'If you refuse to trust him with the petty cash box, *a fortiori* you must not let him handle our bank deposits.'


**a fronte praecipitium a tergo lupi**
between the devil and the deep blue sea

*A fronte praecipitium a tergo lupi* is literally 'a precipice in front, wolves behind'. What to do when caught between equally hazardous or difficult alternatives.


**age quod agis**
pay attention to what you are doing

*Age quod agis*, literally 'Do what you are doing', is excellent advice for those who become careless in their work as well as for those who fail to do what they are supposed to do.


**Agnus Dei**
Lamb of God

*Agnus Dei*, the epithet applied to Christ by John the Baptist, is represented in the figure of a lamb supporting a cross or a banner with a cross emblazoned on it. The lamb, often shown with a halo about its head, represents Christ. A medallion stamped with this figure and blessed by the Pope is also an *Agnus Dei*. The words *Agnus Dei*, translated as 'O Lamb of God', are heard in the office for burial of the dead in the Catholic Mass, and the music for this part of the service is called an *Agnus Dei*.

## a latere
from the side

Cardinals in the particular confidence of a pope – having the ear of the pope – are said to be *a latere* cardinals. A papal emissary enjoying such confidence is called *legatus a latere*. In a broader sense, any person who is a close adviser to an important official can be given the informal appellation *a latere*, implying power for the adviser and status for the official. In government, a plenipotentiary may be thought of as a *legatus a latere*. *A latere* is also used in law, with the meaning 'collateral', in describing succession to property.


## albae gallinae filius
a lucky devil

*Albae gallinae filius*, literally 'a son of a white hen', found its meaning in a Roman folktale. An eagle was said to have dropped a white hen into the lap of Livia, the wife of Emperor Augustus. This remarkable incident was interpreted by soothsayers as a favourable omen, since white hens were believed to bring good fortune. We refer to a particular type of lucky fellow as someone 'born with a silver spoon in his mouth', and the phrase *albae gallinae filius* may be used in this sense as well.


## albo lapillo notare diem
to mark a day with a white stone

Colours have symbolic meanings in all cultures. For the Romans, white was the symbol of happiness, black of misfortune. Thus, in a trial a vote for acquittal was cast with a white stone, for condemnation a black one; a happy day was marked with a white stone, an unhappy day with a black one. The latter procedure was this: at the end of each day, a Roman – according to Pliny the Younger, this superstitious practice dated back to the Thracians – would judge whether the day had been happy or unhappy. Once decided, the Roman would drop a pebble of the appropriate colour into an urn, so at the end of a month he could empty the urn and be able to look back over the month past. (See *nigro notanda lapillo*.) We still speak of red-letter days, so why not an *albo lapillo*, a white-stone day?

**alea iacta est**
the die is cast

Julius Caesar, preparing in 49 BC to enter Rome from Gaul, where he was governor, came to the Rubicon, the river that marked the boundary between Cisalpine Gaul and Italy. Caesar knew that once he crossed the Rubicon he would be in great danger, since he would be seen as defying his government. Suetonius reported that Caesar, anxious over the possible effects of the move he was considering, on the night before making his decision saw an apparition that impelled him to take the warlike step. Plutarch gave a different account: on the night before the crossing Caesar was so troubled by the gravity of his contemplated action against the mother country that he dreamed he had sexual intercourse with his own mother. Both sources do agree, however, that when Caesar finally made up his mind to move boldly, he said, '*Iacta alea est*', a common phrase of the time. Even today, 'The die is cast' means that a bold and irretrievable decision has been made. Caesar's decision eventually resulted in triumph. Those who know only the English translation of *alea iacta* (or *iacta alea*) *est* may think erroneously that *alea* refers to another kind of 'die' rather than the singular form of 'dice'. It is also worth pointing out that in English 'to cross the Rubicon' is to commit oneself to a hazardous enterprise by taking a decisive action that cannot be undone.

**alere flammam**
to feed the flame

Ovid spoke of *alere flammas*, 'to feed the flames', in a figurative sense, which is the intention today whenever we say *alere flammam* or *alere flammas*. 'Further discussion on this matter will only serve *alere flammam*.' One may also use these phrases when speaking of rekindling feelings of love, ambition and the like. Old flames never die?

**alias dictus**
otherwise called

The full ancestor of the English word 'alias', with the meaning 'an assumed name'. As a Latin word, *alias* can be translated as 'at another time'. While our own use of *alias* usually limits its application to circumstances less than honourable – in contrast with 'pen name' and 'stage name' – the Romans did not intend this. They used *alias dictus* in referring to someone's nickname, employed without any interest in deception. In modern law, the expression may be used in much the same way as 'also known as' (abbreviated aka) is employed. 'Schmidt *alias dictus* Smith owned the business for only two months.'

**alieni generis**
of a different kind

**alieni iuris** (or **juris**)
subject to another's authority

*Alieni iuris*, a term in law, literally means 'of another's law'. When, for example, a court places an infant (someone below the legal age of maturity) or a mentally incompetent person under control of a guardian, the infant or incompetent person is said to be *alieni iuris*. Those who are *alieni iuris* cannot exercise control of their ordinary legal rights but must submit to the authority of appointed guardians.

**aliquando bonus dormitat Homerus**
you can't win 'em all

A modification, literally 'Sometimes even good Homer sleeps', of Horace's line concerning Homer (see *quandoque bonus dormitat Homerus*). The intention is that even the best of writers do not always write well, or more broadly, even the greatest in any field are not always up to form. This is said to excuse one's own less than perfect efforts or to criticize gently the work of another that is not up to usual quality.

**alis volat propriis**
she (he) flies on her (his) own wings

The intention is clear: he or she has an independent spirit. In line with today's enlightened parenthood, a parent watching proudly as a child manages independently can say *alis volat propriis*. The Latin gives no indication of gender, so the statement can be made of any newly independent offspring. The translation 'she flies on her own wings' reflects the customs of a less enlightened day, when gender was applied to ships of state as well as to other ships. (For the crossword puzzle fan, it is worth mentioning that *ala* means 'wing'.)

## alma mater
nourishing mother

*Alma mater* is the epithet applied by Romans to Ceres, goddess of growing vegetation, to Cybele, a nature goddess, and to other bounteous goddesses. Roman poets referred to the country of their birth as *alma mater*. Today the expression is used to refer to one's college or university and, more narrowly, to the official song, statue or other symbol of the institution. (See *alumnus*.)

## alter ego
bosom pal

Literally translated as 'another I' or 'another self', an *alter ego* is an inseparable friend. The intention is that an *alter ego* may be considered as speaking or acting for the other person. Another way of conveying the same thought is given in the next phrase, *alter idem*, which is far less common.

## alter idem
another self

Cicero used the expression **tamquam alter idem**, 'as if a second self', to describe a completely trustworthy friend, an *alter ego*. *Idem* means 'the same', while *ego* means 'I', but both phrases convey the same meaning. Anyone who is your *alter idem* or *alter ego* is your inseparable friend.

## altissima quaeque flumina minimo sono labi
still waters run deep

Literally 'The deepest rivers flow with the least sound', this Roman proverb suggests that we not sell short those who eschew self-promotion, at the same time cautioning us to watch out for people given to blowing their own horns.

**alumnus**
nursling, foster child

We all know the English word 'alumnus' as a graduate or former student of an academic institution, and even of an institution not commonly thought of as academic, so it is interesting to understand the Latin *alumnus*, with the meanings given above. When we understand *alumnus* in its Roman intention, we can better understand the idea of *alma mater* as 'nourishing mother'. The plural of *alumnus* is *alumni*, the feminine is *alumna*, the feminine plural *alumnae*.


**amantes sunt amentes**
lovers are lunatics

The foolish things that lovers do are considered justification for this maxim. In *A Midsummer Night's Dream*, Shakespeare's Theseus puts it thus:
    The lunatic, the lover and the poet
    Are of imagination all compact.
Those of us who still have our wits will take this into account when we are smitten. After all, Publilius Syrus advised us that **amare et sapere vix deo conceditur**, 'Even a god finds it hard to love and be wise at the same time.'


**amantium irae amoris integratio est**
lovers' quarrels are the renewal of love

How much truth there is in this old Roman proverb is anyone's guess, but Terence is the source for this insight, and others have picked it up. Robert Frost said in one poem that he would choose as an epitaph: 'I had a lover's quarrel with the world.' What better way to express one's love affair with life? (See *qui bene amat bene castigat* for further wisdom.)


**a maximis ad minima**
from the greatest to the least

This expression refers to objects or abstractions, not people. 'She concerned herself with all of society's problems, *a maximis ad minima.*'

**a mensa et toro**
a legal separation

*A mensa et toro*, with the literal meaning of 'from table and bed', is found in the legal phrase 'divorce *a mensa et toro*', referring to a decree forbidding husband and wife to share living quarters. *Mensa* is translated in this construction as 'a table for dining', but it also means 'altar' or 'sacrificial table' in other uses, as well as 'a table used by moneychangers' for doing their business. Those with a cynical attitude toward marriage and divorce thus might well read cruel humour into a divorce *a mensa et toro*. Even more ironic is the meaning of *torus*, from which we have the form *toro*. *Torus* has many meanings, one of which is 'bed' and another 'marriage couch', but in other contexts it carries the meaning of 'bier'.

**amicus curiae**
an impartial spokesman in a court of law

An *amicus curiae*, literally 'friend of the court', is a person not party to a litigation who volunteers or is invited by the court to give advice on a matter pending before it.

**amicus humani generis**
a philanthropist

Literally 'a friend of the human race'.

**amicus usque ad aras**
a friend to the end

Literally 'a friend as far as to the altars', this expression can be taken as 'a friend unto death', but it is also interpreted as 'a friend up to the point where friendship conflicts with religious or ethical beliefs'. Pericles of Athens is said to have responded in this latter sense when refusing to swear falsely for a friend.

**amor**
love

The word used to express fondness or passion. (See the next four entries.)

**amor nummi**
cupidity

Literally 'love of money'. (See *radix omnium malorum est cupiditas*.)

**amor patriae**
patriotism

Literally 'love of country'.

**amor proximi**
love of one's neighbour

Leviticus adjures 'Love thy neighbour as thyself'. At the same time, we must be careful not to covet our neighbour's wife.

**amor vincit omnia**
love conquers all

This famous line of Virgil's (also given, to the despair of beginning Latin students, unaccustomed to the flexibility of Latin word order, as **amor omnia vincit** or as **omnia vincit amor**) is quoted by Chaucer in the 'Prologue' to *The Canterbury Tales*. Incidentally, Virgil goes on to say, **et nos cedamus amori**, 'and let us yield to it [love]'.

**anguis in herba**
a hidden danger

Literally 'a snake in the grass'. Virgil, in his *Eclogues*, used the expression **latet anguis in herba**, 'A snake lies concealed in the grass', to call attention to a hidden danger. The danger may be of any type, even though the English 'snake in the grass' is usually a person who has turned against his friend, particularly an adulterer who has taken up with the friend's wife.

**animal bipes implume**
a human being

Literally 'a two-legged animal without feathers', *animal bipes implume* is the Latin translation of Plato's definition of man, and thus a contemptuous designation for *homo sapiens* (literally 'wise man', itself a world-class self-serving expression). Two other uses of *animal* are worthy of note here. **Animal disputans** is 'an argumentative person', and **animal rationale** is 'a reasoning person', and like *animal bipes implume*, both may be translated as 'a human being'.

### animis opibusque parati
ready for anything

Literally meaning 'prepared in minds and resources'. Any prudent person is always *animis opibusque parati*, but this saying has special application for those who embark on a new adventure, and it may also serve those who anticipate the unpredictable final adventure of all mortals, as any life insurance salesman will tell you.

### anno aetatis suae ...
in the year of his (or her) age ...

This is the full expression often given as *aetatis suae*. It is seen on tombstones as well as in old texts and family Bibles, often abbreviated AAS: 'Died AAS 64.'

### anno Domini
in the year of our Lord

The full version of the abbreviation AD. Modern Western calendars reckon passage of time from the birth of Christ, the commencement of the Christian era, but there is disagreement over the precise year of Christ's birth. (See the next four entries.)

### anno hegirae
in the year of the hegira

AD 622 is the year in which Mahomet fled from Mecca to Medina, and the month is generally given as September, so it is AD 622 that is taken as the beginning of the Muslim era, the precise date for its first day corresponding to 16 July 622. The Arabic word for 'flight' is *hijirah*, from which came the Latin word *hegira* and then the English word 'hegira'. To commemorate Mahomet's flight,

Muslims make the same journey as a pilgrimage. *Anno hegirae* is abbreviated AH in giving dates in the Muslim calendar. 1421 AH will commence early in AD 2000.

## anno mundi
in the year of the world

Yet another term for reckoning passage of time from a fixed event. *Anno mundi*, abbreviated AM, marks the number of years that have passed since the world began. In the Hebrew tradition, the year of creation corresponds to 3761 BC. The Irish theologian Ussher in the mid-seventeenth century computed the date of creation as 4004 BC. Thus, the year AD 2000 will correspond to 5761 AM or 6004 AM, depending on whose date of creation is preferred.

## anno regni
in the year of the reign

Abbreviated AR, *anno regni* is used to mark the passage of years in the riegn of a monarch.

## anno urbis conditae
in the year since Rome was founded

For Romans, 'the City', *urbs*, was Rome, so *anno urbis conditae*, literally 'in the year of the founded city', refers to the number of years that have passed since 753 BC, the traditional date of the founding of Rome. (See *ab urbe condita*.)

## annuit coeptis
He (God) has favoured our undertaking

This saying, from Virgil's *Aeneid*, appears on the reverse of the great seal of the United States, which can be seen on the reverse of the United States $1 bill. By employing *annuit coeptis* in this way, the USA joins many other countries in suggesting that God takes a special interest in particular societies. (See *e pluribus unum* and *novus ordo seclorum*.)

## annus mirabilis
a remarkable year

Any year in which great events occur may be called an *annus mirabilis*, for example AD 1666, when a great fire raged in London for almost a week and virtually destroyed that city. The phrase is also used to designate a year in which figures of great importance were born, particularly when that year produced important people in great numbers. Thus, the year 1809 is considered an *annus mirabilis*. Consider first Charles Darwin and Abraham Lincoln, who were born in that year, and then go on to Alfred, Lord Tennyson, and to Nikolai Gogol, Oliver Wendell Holmes, Edgar Allan Poe and Felix Mendelssohn, as well as Louis Braille, Edward FitzGerald, William Gladstone, Fanny Kemble and even Kit Carson.

## ante bellum
before the war

The period before any war may be characterized as *ante bellum*, but in the United States the phrase generally is applied to the period before the Civil War. In English, 'antebellum' is used as an adjective with the meaning 'pre-war': 'The antebellum South is looked back upon with great nostalgia by some Americans.'

## ante Christum
before Christ

Abbreviated AC (See *anno Domini*.)

## ante meridiem
before noon

*Meridies* means 'noon' or 'midday'. The English abbreviation for *ante meridiem*, a.m., refers to time prior to noon and after midnight. (See *post meridiem*.)

## ante mortem
before death

*Ante mortem*, abbreviated AM but not to be confused with *anno mundi* or with *ante meridiem* which have the same abbreviation, is an easily understood phrase that refers to the period in which death is imminent. The phrase has fathered an English adjective, 'antemortem': an antemortem statement is a deathbed statement and therefore is given great weight in a court of law, since a person who knows death is near is presumed to have no reason to tell anything but the truth.

### ante partum
before childbirth

The period before childbirth may be described as *ante partum*. (See *post partum*.)

### apage Satanas
away with thee, Satan

The concept of Satan as the archfiend is part of the Judaeo-Christian tradition. The meaning of the noun *satan* in Hebrew, from which we work through Greek to find our way to *Satanas* in Latin, is 'adversary', and we still contend with Satan today. Jesus said: 'Get thee behind me, Satan.' Today, with a little Latin, anyone confronted by temptation may say, '*Apage Satanas*'.

### apologia pro vita sua
a defence of his life

An *apologia* is especially a written justification for one's opinions or actions. John Henry Newman, the celebrated Anglican theologian who converted to Catholicism in 1845, wrote *Apologia Pro Vita Sua* (1864), his religious autobiography, in which he defends the things he did in his life by way of explaining the basis for his faith. He was made a cardinal in 1879. Anyone can write an *apologia pro vita sua*, but it is clear that any such attempt will be looked upon as effrontery in light of Cardinal Newman's accomplishment, which is considered a literary masterpiece.

### a posse ad esse
from the possible to the actual

Turning an idea or a dream into reality.

## a posteriori
from effect to cause

Reasoning *a posteriori*, literally 'from what comes after', is a logical process in which propositions are derived from the observation of facts or in which principles are established from generalizations based on facts. Thus, *a posteriori* reasoning, also called 'inductive reasoning', is based initially on experience. (See *a priori*.)

## apparatus criticus
critical matter

This modern Latin expression, sometimes written **criticus apparatus**, is used to designate supplementary scholarly information, such as variant readings or notes, intended to assist the serious reader of a text. Often abbreviated *apparatus*, explanatory information of this type can have such great bulk that the original text is dwarfed by it, to the delight of the editor and the dismay of the less than devoted reader. 'The Yale Edition of Samuel Johnson's works is noted for the completeness of its *apparatus criticus*.'

## a priori
from what is already known

Reasoning *a priori*, literally 'from what comes before', is a logical process in which consequences are deduced from principles that are assumed. Thus, *a priori* reasoning, also called 'deductive reasoning', is based initially on assumptions that derive from prior knowledge. (See *a posteriori*.)

## aqua et igni interdictus
banished

This expression may be translated as 'forbidden water and fire'. Caesar and Cicero used **interdicere alicui** ('to deny to someone') **aqua et igni**, as an expression meaning 'to banish'. A banished person is denied society; that is, no member of the community may provide him with life's necessities.

**aqua pura**
distilled water

Literally 'pure water'.

**aqua vitae**
whisky

Literally 'water of life', *aqua vitae*, originally an alchemist's term, appears to be the most amusing euphemism ever invented for hard liquor. Yet no one would deny that *aqua vitae* at times is literally just what its name promises. Physicians are said to carry spirits in their bags, ready for use as restoratives, and formidable amounts of strong drink have been used in Hollywood movies to anaesthetize patients about to undergo emergency surgery. The Scandinavians, perhaps because of their long, hard winters, may have been even more justified than the Romans in calling spirits *aqua vitae*. They came up with *akvavit*, a gin-like liquor flavoured with caraway seeds (the alternative spelling of *akvavit* is *aquavit*). But an additional word must be said of the origin of the word *whisky*: it derives ultimately from the Irish and Scottish Gaelic *uisage beatha*, and what does this phrase mean? 'Water of life'.

**a quo**
from which

**arbiter bibendi**
a toastmaster

Literally 'the judge of the drinking', an *arbiter bibendi* in Roman times was much more than a mere toastmaster, as we know the latter term today. Whereas the principal duty of a toastmaster is to preside at a banquet, introducing after-dinner speakers and those who propose toasts, the *arbiter bibendi* kept an eye on the amount of wine drunk at feasts, giving special attention to the proportion of water added to the wine to bring it down to a reasonable strength. In classical times, only the dissolute drank wine at full strength.

## arbiter elegantiae
an authority in matters of taste

Anyone established as *arbiter elegantiae* or *arbiter elegantiarum* is considered the last word in matters of elegance or style.

## Arcades ambo
two of a kind

Virgil, in his *Eclogues*, wrote of *Arcades ambo*, literally 'Arcadians both', two men of exceptional skill in pastoral poetry and music. Ancient Arcadia, in the Peloponnesus, was perceived as a region of rustic simplicity and contentment, where poetry and music flourished. Thus, in one sense, *Arcades ambo* may be taken as 'two persons having like tastes, characteristics, or professions'. But the expression has another interpretation: in *Don Juan*, Lord Byron used the phrase ironically: '*Arcades ambo, id est* – blackguards both.' Byron's intention has overtaken Virgil's, so *Arcades ambo* today more often is used pejoratively.

## arcanum arcanorum
secret of secrets

The ultimate secret, the secret of nature that supposedly underlies the work of the alchemist, astrologer and magician.

## argumentum
an argument or proof or appeal

Rhetoric was important to the Romans, so they had many phrases in which *argumentum* was combined with other terms, as can be seen by reading on below. It must be made clear here that *argumentum* is not a disagreement but a proof, especially one adduced to illuminate or clarify.

## argumentum ab auctoritate
a proof derived from authority

## argumentum ab inconvenienti
an appeal based on the hardship or inconvenience involved

**argumentum ad absurdum**

an appeal pointing out the absurdity of one's opponent's point of view, rather than establishing the merits of one's own position

(See *reductio ad absurdum.*)


**argumentum ad captandum**

an appeal based primarily on arousing popular passions

(See *ad captandum vulgus.*)


**argumentum ad crumenam**

an appeal based on money or the promise of profit

A *crumena*, a leather pouch that held money, was secured by a strap around a Roman's neck. Thus the meaning of *argumentum ad crumenam* as an appeal to the pocketbook – and what is more convincing?


**argumentum ad hominem**

an argument against the man

*Argumentum ad hominem* is an effective rhetorical tactic, appealing to feelings rather than intellect, or directed against an opponent's character rather than the subject under discussion. *Argumentum ad hominem* is considered a logical fallacy, in that such an argument fails to prove a point by failing to address it. There is no doubt, however, that in practical politics and in many a court of law, *argumentum ad hominem* is persuasive. (See *ad rem* and *argumentum ad rem.*)


**argumentum ad invidiam**

an appeal to envy or other undesirable human traits

A powerful tool for the demagogue.


**argumentum ad rem**

a relevant argument

See *ad rem.*

**argumentum baculinum**
an appeal to force

*Argumentum baculinum* has long been a popular and effective form of persuasion. In *Argumentum baculinum*, the force is suggested by wielding a walking stick (*baculum*), but a *baculum* was also the sceptre that symbolized magisterial authority, so the force implied may also be that of governmental authority or legal compulsion.

**arma virumque cano**
arms and the man I sing

The opening words of Virgil's great epic poem, the *Aeneid*. In an epic, a hero has many demanding adventures, which the poet describes in elevated style. The *Aeneid* traces the experiences of Aeneas, defender of Troy, after the destruction of Troy, in the legendary war precipitated by Helen's abduction by Paris in about 1200 BC.

**arrectis auribus**
on the alert

Literally 'with ears pricked up'. While the phrase describes the characteristic appearance of an animal intent on finding or fighting its prey, it can be used in giving advice to our friends: 'In the city, ever *arrectis auribus*.'

**ars amandi**
art of love

Literally 'the art of loving'.

**Ars Amatoria**
The Art of Love

The title of Ovid's work on the amatory art, with full accounts of how to find and keep a lover. This how-to book of ancient Rome – it was published about 2 BC – is still worth reading. Within a few years after *Ars Amatoria* appeared, Ovid was banished from Rome by Emperor Augustus, and he died an exile in AD 17. Ovid, in his autobiographical work *Tristia*, gives two reasons for his exile:

*carmen*, 'song', and *error*, an unspecified 'indiscretion'. From his extended justifications in *Tristia* and other late works, it is clear that Ovid believed *Ars Amatoria* had offended the prudish Augustus.


### ars artium
logic

Literally 'the art of arts'.


### ars est celare artem
true art conceals the means by which it is achieved

Ovid's maxim in *Ars Amatoria*, literally 'It is art to conceal art', has it that in the best works of art the audience is not distracted by the artist's technique but responds instead to the power of the work, as the artist intended. True art must appear artless. *Ars est celare artem* as a critical evaluation of a work of art is thus a high compliment.


### ars gratia artis
art for art's sake

The motto of the true artist, now pre-empted by Hollywood: Metro-Goldwyn-Mayer, the film-producers, use it as part of the MGM trademark.


### ars longa, vita brevis
art is long, but life is short

The Greek physician Hippocrates coined this aphorism, here given in its Latin translation, telling us that the art of healing has a life much longer than that of its practitioner (and patient, we might add), but *ars longa, vita brevis* is generally extended to all the arts today. The principal intent, no matter how *ars* is interpreted, is to point out that we are mortal and must anticipate death. Longfellow, in his 'Psalm of Life', put it this way for all of us:

> Art is long, and Time is fleeting,
> And our hearts, though stout and brave,
> Still, like muffled drums, are beating
> Funeral marches to the grave.

A sobering thought.

## ars moriendi
the art of dying

The Romans put much store in dying nobly. (See *paete, non dolet.*)

## ars poetica
the art of poetry

Also the title, *Ars Poetica*, of an epistolary poem of Horace, written about 20 BC, expounding his literary theory.

## arte perire sua
to trip oneself up

Here – recall the English adjective 'artful', as in the Artful Dodger in *Oliver Twist* – *ars* takes on a meaning akin to wiles or cunning or machinations, so a literal translation of *arte perire sua* is 'to perish by one's own machinations'. The expression is not unlike our own 'hoist with his own petard', 'blown up by his own bomb', but understood as 'trapped by his own machinations'.

## artes perditae
lost arts

Any skills forgotten by a culture are *artes perditae*. 'Addition and multiplication, as a trip to any supermarket will demonstrate, are *artes perditae*.'

## Artium Baccalaureus
Bachelor of Arts

Abbreviated AB or BA. This, of course, is the undergraduate degree awarded by colleges and universities. The derivation of the term is not clear. It has been suggested that the medieval Latin term *baccalaureus*, 'bachelor', was adapted from *baccalarius*, meaning 'labourer' or 'tenant'. This discussion is intended solely to suggest the possibly humble origin of the bachelor of arts degree, awarded formally after three years' hard labour.

### Artium Magister
Master of Arts

Abbreviated AM or MA. A higher university degree.

### asinus asinum fricat
one fool rubs the other's back

Two people who lavish excessive praise on one another – perhaps no one else sees anything praiseworthy in either of them – exemplify *asinus asinum fricat*, literally 'The ass rubs the ass'. No group has a corner on the market for *asinus asinum fricat*. Wherever people of small talent gather, someone sooner or later will establish a chapter of the Mutual Admiration Society.

### astra castra, numen lumen
the stars my camp, God my lamp

### a tergo
from behind

This expression is applied most often today to a position in sexual intercourse in which the male lies behind the female.

### auctor ignotus
an unknown author

Not a put-down. An *auctor ignotus* is an author whose work has not gained the recognition it merits.

### audaces fortuna iuvat (or juvat)
fortune favours the bold

Also given as **audentes** ('the daring') **fortuna iuvat**. This motto for the bold and successful and for those who aspire to success was cited by many Roman writers. The English proverb 'Nothing ventured, nothing gained' captures the spirit of this common Roman saying.

**audi alteram partem**
there are two sides to every question

Literally 'Hear the other side'. A plea for reason and fairness in discussion.

**aura popularis**
temporary celebrity

Cicero's expression for the public's favourite at a particular time, who is said to be enjoying *aura popularis*, literally 'the popular breeze'. But breezes subside.

**aurea mediocritas**
moderation in all things

Those of us who are satisfied with lives of security and contentment seek *aurea mediocritas*, literally 'the golden mean'. We are willing to live out our days without taking great risks, without indulging in excesses. *Aurea mediocritas* is an expression used by Horace, in his *Odes*; he intended it in the meaning just described: 'Who loves the golden mean is safe from the poverty of a hovel and free from the envy of a palace.'

**aureo hamo piscari**
money talks

Literally 'to fish with a golden hook', *aureo hamo piscari* recognizes the marvellous persuasiveness of cash on the nail. This is not unlike **auro quaeque ianua panditur**, which we know as 'A golden key opens any door' but which translates literally as 'Any door is opened by means of gold'.

**auri sacra fames**
money-mad

Those who live only to acquire wealth are characterized by Virgil as having *auri sacra fames*, literally 'the cursed hunger for gold'.

**Aurora**
goddess of the morning

In Roman mythology, Aurora was responsible for such duties as extinguishing stars at the end of night. But there was more to her:

she had a weakness for mortal men, her favourite being Tithonus, son of the king of Troy. After stealing him away, she inveigled Jupiter into giving Tithonus immortality but neglected to arrange for eternal youth for the poor fellow. In time, he grew old and unappealing, so Aurora locked him in his room. All that was heard from Tithonus from then on was a feeble cry from time to time. As a final act of mercy, Aurora turned him into a grasshopper. We know Aurora today mostly in the terms *aurora australis* and *aurora borealis*, the southern lights and northern lights, which delight and mystify us.

### auspicium melioris aevi
an omen of a better time

Yet another expression revealing the Romans' deep concern with auguries. Finding a white stone, a flower growing in a rock or any other sign of good things to come – *auspicium melioris aevi* – was taken quite seriously.

### Austriae est imperare orbi universo
It is Austria's destiny to rule the world

The motto of Emperor Frederick III, one of the Hapsburgs. The fact that the Hapsburgs no longer dictate to anybody, not even the Austrians, is a commentary on the impermanence of power. The abbreviation of Frederick's motto, whether rendered in German or in Latin, is itself worthy of mention: AEIOU is the abbreviation of the German *Alles Erdreich ist Oesterreich unterthan*, 'The whole world is subjected to Austria', retaining for moderns the irony as well as the initial letters of the Latin phrase.

### aut bibat aut abeat
you're either for us or against us

This saying, a borrowing from the Greek, in the literal sense is taken as 'Let him either drink or depart'. In an extended meaning, *aut bibat aut abeat* can be used to force participation on an unwilling member of a plan or conspiracy. Either the hesitating fellow goes along with the others or he is no longer welcome.

**aut Caesar aut nihil**
all or nothing

Literally 'either Caesar (that is, emperor of Rome) or nothing', associated with Julius Caesar, who said he would sooner be number one man in a village than number two in Rome. Also a motto of Cesare Borgia (1476–1507), the favourite son of Pope Alexander VI, who was known for his crimes and violence, even against members of his own family. One of his lovable practices, according to legend, was that of poisoning the wine of rivals before joining them in toasting mutual friendship. Borgia's failure to achieve his ambition to seize total power reflects badly on the efficacy of his underhanded methods. *Aut Caesar aut nihil* is also given as **aut Caesar aut nullus** ('nobody'), with the same meaning.

**aut disce aut discede**
either learn or leave

A suitable motto for a school sufficiently principled, not to mention well endowed, to be able to insist on excellent academic standards.

**aut viam inveniam aut faciam**
where there's a will there's a way

Literally 'I'll either find a way or make one', *aut viam inveniam aut faciam* is the credo of the person who plugs along, unwilling ever to admit defeat. Such a person is determined, not obstinate.

**aut vincere aut mori**
victory or death

A Roman motto, literally 'either to conquer or to die', intended to inspire soldiers preparing for battle, also found (in French) in a stanza of the *Marseillaise*. Gilbert and Sullivan mock this spirit in their *Pirates of Penzance*, where the fair young maidens exhort the departing constabulary to fight bravely against the threatening pirates: 'Go, ye heroes, go and die.' Anyone who has ever prepared for battle will understand the effectiveness of such encouragement.

**ave atque vale**
hail and farewell

*Ave*, 'hail', was the Roman equivalent of 'hello', and *vale* the equivalent of 'goodbye', as well as the Roman farewell to the dead. Catullus used this expression in closing a poem on the death of his brother: '**Atque in perpetuum, frater, ave atque vale.**' 'And forever, brother, hail and farewell!'

**ave Caesar, morituri te salutant**
hail, Caesar, those who are about to die salute you

A line suitable for the clever schoolboy making his appearance before a board of examiners. The words are those of Roman gladiators entering the arena to launch into mortal combat. Suetonius tells us in his *Lives of the Caesars* that Emperor Claudius (AD 41–54) so enjoyed these spectacles that he ordered that even those who fell accidentally be put to death. He wanted to watch their faces as they died. No wonder the gladiators referred to themselves as 'those who are about to die'. The full expression is also given as **Ave, Caesar, morituri te salutamus,** 'Hail, Caesar, we who are about to die salute you.'

**ave Maria**
hail' Mary

The angel's salutation to the Virgin, from Luke's Gospel.

**a verbis ad verbera**
from words to blows

An expression useful in describing a discussion that is heating up.

**Ave Regina Caelorum**
Hail, Queen of Heaven

Title of a hymn in honour of the Virgin, the Queen of Heaven.

**a vinculo matrimonii**
an absolute divorce

A divorce *a vinculo matrimonii*, literally 'from the bond of marriage', and also called a divorce *a vinculo*, is one that releases husband and wife from all legal commitments of marriage. It is interesting to note that *vinculum*, 'bond', also means 'noose' and 'chain'.

**beatae memoriae**
of blessed memory

Used on tombstones and memorial plaques.


**Beata Maria**
Blessed Mary

Maria, of course, is the Virgin Mary. Other Latin expressions are also used in referring to Mary, including **Beata Virgo** (Blessed Virgin) and **Beata Virgo Maria** (Blessed Virgin Mary). The abbreviations BM and BV for *Beata Maria* and *Beata Virgo* are sometimes seen.


**beati pacifici**
blessed are the peacemakers

In Matthew's Gospel the opening words of the eighth beatitude of the Sermon on the Mount, concluding 'for they shall be called sons of God'.


**beati pauperes spiritu**
blessed are the poor in spirit

In Matthew's Gospel, the opening words of the Sermon on the Mount, concluding 'for theirs is the kingdom of heaven'. The irrepressible Alexander Pope wrote a beatitude of his own: 'Blessed is the man who expects nothing, for he shall never be disappointed.'

**beati possidentes**
possession is nine points of the law

Literally 'blessed are those who possess' (for they shall receive). This expression finds its principal meaning in conveying the idea that one may claim property most easily before the law when one has physical possession of it – consider the long-time squatter on land deeded to another person. In a cynical vein, *beati possidentes*, translated literally, may be taken as a commentary on the uncanny knack of the haves to acquire even more, while the have-nots acquire even less.

**beatus**
the blessed person

See *advocatus diaboli*.

**bellum**
war

An important word in the expansionist Roman world, but not always looked upon with favour: Horace wrote of **bella detesta matribus**, 'wars, the horror of mothers', and Virgil wrote of **bella horrida bella**, 'wars, horrid wars'.

**bene**
well

A noteworthy observation incorporating this adverb is **bene qui latuit bene vixit**, literally 'He who has lived in obscurity has lived well'. The line is from *Tristia*, Ovid's extended lament about his enforced exile from Rome, and its meaning is not to be taken as a panegyric for the simple life. Rather, Ovid is expressing bitterness over the way things have turned out for him, telling us that the powerful – Emperor Augustus *et al.* – are envious of brilliance and attractiveness in others, so *bene qui latuit bene vixit*, 'Keep a low profile if you wish to survive'. Whistle-blowers, beware.

**beneficium accipere libertatem est vendere**
to accept a favour is to sell one's freedom

In *Hamlet*, Polonius advises his son:
　　Neither a borrower, nor a lender be;
　　For loan oft loses both itself and friend,
　　And borrowing dulls the edge of husbandry.

So much for Shakespeare's wisdom on extending kindness as well as receiving it. Let's turn to a Roman playwright. *Beneficium accipere libertatem est vendere*, a maxim attributed to Publilius Syrus, recognizes only the problems of those on the receiving end. And the New Testament? The Acts of the Apostles: 'It is more blessed to give than to receive.' So traditional sources of wisdom appear to agree that acts of kindness may lead to misery rather than to improvement in the quality of our lives, and we are left confused and uncertain. Perhaps everything depends on the spirit in which we give and the terms under which we borrow.


**bis dat qui cito dat**
he gives twice who quickly gives

This Latin proverb, quoted by Cervantes in *Don Quixote*, may serve as a fitting motto for professional fund-raisers, who so often have to badger self-professed donors into delivering on their pledges. There is little joy in such gifts, nor is there satisfaction in any act of charity or kindness given reluctantly and only after repeated appeals.


**bis repetita placent**
a little originality, please

A derogatory comment, literally 'The things that please are those that are asked for again and again', appropriate for a derivative work. Horace was telling us in *bis repetita placent* that certain works of art please once, but others, tried and true, are imitated widely and always please. Thus, when we see a work obviously patterned after a previous successful work, we may say *bis repetita placent* or merely *bis repetita*, telling·the creator of the imitative work that he is catering to the public's taste rather than attempting something original.

**bis vivit qui bene vivit**
he lives twice who lives well

Milton, in *Paradise Lost*, couched the same wisdom in these words:

> Nor love thy life, nor hate; but what thou liv'st
> Live well; how long or short permit to Heaven.

So we are being told that quality of life is much more important than longevity. But *bis vivit qui bene vivit*, besides counselling us to lead productive lives, offers a consoling thought to recall when a friend dies young.

**bona fide**
in good faith

This phrase can also be translated as 'honestly', 'sincerely' or with any other word or expression denoting 'without deception'. *Bona fide* has been used as an adjective phrase in our own language so often that we all know it by its English pronunciation. To produce *bona fides* means to show good intentions in dealing with others, show credentials, prove one's identity or ability etc. No fraud or deceit is intended or shown. (See *mala fide*.)

**bonis avibus**
under favourable signs

Literally 'under good birds', a phrase indicating that the omens are favourable for a contemplated action. The Romans relied so heavily on birds, *aves*, as tools in divination that the noun *avis* is translated as 'sign' or 'omen' as well as 'bird', and *avi mala* and *avi sinistra* mean 'bad omens'. But the Romans were not the only ones who found magic in birds. Consider, for example, the persistent use of the dove as a symbol of peace, innocence and love.

**bonum vinum laetificat cor hominis**
good wine gladdens a person's heart

The Psalms speak of 'wine that maketh glad the heart of man', referring to the bountiful favours provided by God. In the modern world, *bonum vinum laetificat* may find wider application as a slogan for promoting consumption of wine and spirits.

**brutum fulmen**
an empty threat

*Brutum fulmen*, literally 'an insensible thunderbolt', reminds us of Pliny's phrase **bruta fulmina et vana**, 'thunderbolts that strike blindly and in vain'. Those who argue bombastically or who threaten idly without the inclination or ability to follow up on their threats are said to offer only *brutum fulmen*. One can also apply the phrase to governments that continually threaten their adversaries but never make good on the threats – to the relief of the rest of us, whose sons would be the ones sent to fulfil the threats.

c or **ca.**
See *circa.*

## cacoëthes carpendi
a mania for finding fault

*Cacoëthes*, derived from *kakoethes*, a Greek word that combines *kakos*, 'bad', with *ethos*, 'habit', describes any compulsion or uncontrollable urge. *Cacoëthes* can be used alone to mean 'mania' or 'passion', even 'disease'. With *carpendi*, a form of *carpere*, meaning 'to pluck', as fruit from a tree, the phrase becomes highly useful in describing the uncontrollable urge of an inveterate nitpicker.

## cacoëthes loquendi
compulsive talking

Anyone who goes on talking and talking and talking and talking may be said to exhibit *cacoëthes loquendi.* (See *cacoëthes carpendi.*)

## cacoëthes scribendi
an incurable itch to write

Another form of *cacoëthes.* In the fuller phrase **insanabile** ('incurable') **cacoëthes scribendi**, Juvenal in his *Satires* harshly described the compulsion to write – that is, to become a published writer – still prevalent today. We see the phrase used now as an uncharitable appraisal of a writer deemed untalented, implicitly advising him to abandon writing and pursue some more suitable vocation. Juvenal's full statement is worthy of translation: 'An inveterate and incurable itch for writing besets many and grows old in their sick hearts.' No laughing matter is this incurable itch.

**cadit quaestio**
the argument collapses

*Cadit quaestio*, literally translated as 'the question falls', is said when the central idea of an argument or a legal case collapses: '*Cadit quaestio*, there is nothing further to be said; let us move on to other matters.'

**caeca invidia est**
envy is blind

We are accustomed to thinking of love as blind, but Livy's aphorism *caeca invidia est* tells us that envy also is blind: those possessed by envy overlook facts that would alleviate or eliminate the debilitating condition.

**caeli enarrant gloriam Dei**
the heavens bespeak the glory of God

Often abbreviated *caeli enarrant*, this quotation from the Psalms cites the stars and the planets as brilliant evidence of the wisdom and power of God. *Caeli enarrant* is a fitting expression on seeing the full moon or a particularly spectacular celestial display. *Caeli enarrant* is also a fitting comment – a star is born – on the brilliant début of a musical prodigy, an outstanding new writer or actor or any young person coming to the favourable attention of the public for the first time.

**caelum non animum ...**
See *coelum non animum* ...

**caetera desunt**
the rest are missing

See *cetera desunt*.

**caeteris paribus**
other things being equal

Also given as **ceteris paribus**. 'The President said that *caeteris paribus* he would appoint a woman to the post.'

## Campus Martius
the field of Mars

In the early republic, Romans used the term *Campus Martius* to designate a field on the eastern bank of the Tiber that they used as an encampment when the army was mobilized – Mars, of course, was the Roman god of war. The *Campus Martius* was also used for athletic contests, in themselves a kind of warfare, and for meetings of the *comitia*, the assembly of the Roman people for the election of consuls, magistrates and other officials, as well as to decide on mobilization of the army.

## caput mortuum
worthless residue

The literal meaning of *caput mortuum* is 'death's head', a skull. The term was used by the alchemists to designate the residue in a flask after distillation was complete. *Caput mortuum* now can be taken as any worthless residue, even a useless person.

## caput mundi
the centre of the world

The Romans thought of Rome as *caput mundi*, literally 'the head – the capital – of the world', and perhaps justifiably so. After all, Poe spoke of 'the glory that was Greece and the grandeur that was Rome'. And did not all roads lead to Rome? Those who boost their own hometowns may use *caput mundi* in the same way the Romans did.

## caritas
love, charity

Forgetting that charity designates 'love of humanity', we tend to think of it exclusively as 'giving to the poor'. By *caritas* the Romans meant 'dearness' or 'high price'. (*Carus*, meaning 'dear', is an etymological ancestor of the word 'whore'.) Thus, when Cicero wrote of a year in which the cost of living was high, he used the phrase **annonae caritas**. Eventually *caritas* designated another kind of dearness, the highest love or fellowship – charity as we now know it in the sense conveyed in St Paul's letter to the Corinthians: 'And now abideth faith, hope, charity, these three; but the greatest of these is charity.'

**carpe diem**
enjoy, enjoy

This famous advice, literally, 'Seize the day', is from Horace's *Odes*. The full thought is **carpe diem, quam minimum credula postero**, which may be translated as 'Enjoy today, trusting little in tomorrow'. Thus, *carpe diem* from ancient times until the present has been advice often and variously expressed: enjoy yourself while you have the chance; eat, drink, and be merry, for tomorrow we die; make hay while the sun shines; enjoy yourself, it's later than you think. In another century *carpe diem* was also an exhortation to maidens to give up their virginity and enjoy all the pleasures of life. Robert Herrick (1591–1674):

> Gather ye rosebuds while ye may
> Old Time is still a-flying,
> And this same flower that smiles today
> Tomorrow will be dying.

**carpe hunc librum**
seize this book

Useful advice when offered the chance to benefit from an author's wit and wisdom.

**castigat ridendo mores**
laughter succeeds where lecturing won't

The literal translation of *castigat ridendo mores* is 'It (or he or she) corrects customs (or manners) by laughing at them'. This phrase, therefore, gives us the essence of satire, whose target is the folly of mankind and whose technique is ridicule.

**casus belli**
justification for making war

*Casus* literally means a 'fall' or 'falling', but the word was used by the Romans in many ways, signifying an occasion, opportunity, misfortune, mishap, destruction, downfall etc. Thus Virgil refers to **casus urbis Troianae**, 'the fall of the city of Troy'. *Belli* is the genitive of *bellum* ('war'), and Cicero refers to **bellum domesticum**, 'familial strife', telling us that, alas, marital problems and family disputes are not a recent invention. Historians seek to establish the *casus belli* for each of the many wars that have befallen mankind. Diplomats, we expect, are concerned with avoiding a *casus belli* when relations between nations are strained. But those intent on making war are sure to find a *casus belli* or invent one.

## casus foederis
a situation triggering action under a treaty

*Casus* in its many meanings is discussed under *casus belli*. *Foederis* is the genitive of *foedus* which literally is 'a league' or 'an alliance between two states' but came to mean the document creating the alliance. Those of us who have studied the events leading up to World War I may recall that intricate networks of alliances had been set up among the nations of Europe. When an attack was made on one of the nations so allied, it became the *casus foederis*, obliging all the other nations in one way or another to commit their resources to the tragic war that followed. *Foedus* is not restricted in meaning to alliances between nations. Cicero spoke of **foedus amorum**, 'a love pact', surely a happier and more narrowly intended agreement.

## causa sine qua non
a necessary condition

*Causa sine qua non* is literally 'a cause without which not', so we can readily understand the meaning of the phrase. *Causa* occurs in other phrases as well: **causa causans** can be translated as 'an initiating cause', and **causa causata** as 'a cause owing its existence to a *causa causans* or, perhaps, to another *causa causata*', thus giving us a way to use Latin in arguing the eternal question of who did what to whom first. Theologians use these terms in describing God and His works, God being *causa causans*, and creation *causa causata*.

## caveant consules ne quid detrimenti respublica capiat
beware, consuls, that the republic is not harmed

Usually abbreviated *caveant consules*, 'Consuls beware', this elegant sentence was the formula used by the Roman Senate to invite the consuls – the two chief magistrates of the republic – to designate a dictator in times of crisis. Presumably there was no time available for the ordinary processes of government involving time-consuming debate. In modern use, this formula becomes ominous, alerting a legally constituted government to the threat of replacement by a dictatorship if the people's dissatisfaction with that government is not recognized and reversed.

## caveat emptor
let the buyer beware

The rule of law warning potential purchasers of goods or services that they are not protected during a transaction against failure of the sellers to live up to the bargain except to the extent that the sales contract stipulates. By this rule, the purchaser, not the seller, is responsible for protecting the purchaser in the transaction. *Caveat emptor* is the opposite of **caveat venditor**. Whereas *caveat emptor* has a long history in common law, *caveat venditor* is just now coming into prominence as a result of the consumer rights movement. Under *caveat venditor*, the seller is assumed to be more sophisticated than the purchaser and so must bear responsibility for protecting the unwary purchaser. The purchaser, *emptor*, is a child who must be protected against his own mistakes, while the seller, *venditor*, is the big, bad wolf lying in wait for Little Red Riding Hood. So while the two rules struggle for pre-eminence, lawyers gleefully watch – and litigate.

## cave canem
beware of the dog

This friendly warning, commonly inscribed on doors of Roman homes, was found on the door of a house in Pompeii during excavation of that ancient city, rediscovered in 1748. Pompeii had been buried during an eruption of Mount Vesuvius in AD 79. Finding a homely reminder of the day-to-day lives of an ancient people whose lives were snuffed out suddenly by catastrophe reinforces the validity of the warning found on old clocks: *ultima forsan*, 'perhaps the last hour'. The inhabitants of Pompeii had little warning their time had come. How many of them had followed the injunction *carpe diem*?

**cave quid dicis, quando, et cui**
beware what you say, when and to whom

Excellent advice for all of us. (See *vir sapit qui pauca loquitur*.)

**cedant arma togae**
military power must be subordinate to civil authority

Literally 'Let arms yield to the gown'. Cicero, discussing in *De Officiis* his term as consul, used these words to affirm the primacy of civil authority under his rule, giving us a maxim we may cite to warn against military dictatorship. *Arma*, 'arms', represent the military; *toga*, the garment worn by Roman citizens in their peacetime lives, represents civil authority. (See *toga*.)

**certiorari**
to be made certain

A writ of *certiorari* is a legal document calling for delivery to a higher court of the record of a proceeding before a lower court. The purpose of calling for the record is to enable judicial review of the action taken by the lower court. The basis for issuing the writ is a complaint that an injustice has been done by the lower court.

**certum est quia impossibile est**
it is certain because it is impossible

A maxim of Tertullian (third century AD), in *De Carne Christi*, warning us that in matters of faith we are not to believe the evidence presented to us by our eyes and ears. In light of our limited understanding as mere mortals, the apparent impossibility of the truth of the supernatural is an argument for acceptance, rather than for rejection, of the supernatural.

**cessante causa cessat et effectus**
when the cause is removed, the effect disappears

The validity of *cessante causa cessat et effectus*, literally 'The cause ceasing, the effect also ceases', is demonstrable in most of life's activities, but not in human behaviour, if we are to believe the psychoanalyst. For example, while pain caused by an aching tooth may disappear once the tooth is treated, pain suffered in childhood may plague adults all through their lives.

**cetera desunt**
the rest are missing

This scholarly notation (also given as **caetera desunt**) is used to indicate that parts of a work have not been found despite careful research. 'The full text of the verse by Sappho has never been found, so the missing portions are marked *cetera desunt.*'

**ceteris paribus**
other things being equal

See *caeteris paribus.*

**cf.**
See *confer.*

**circa**
about

This scholar's term abbreviated *c.* or *ca.*, indicates uncertainty about a date. 'It is generally assumed that Chaucer was born *c.* AD 1340.' 'The vase was dated *ca.* fourth century BC.'

**Civis Romanus sum**
I am a Roman citizen

Not everyone in the Roman Empire had citizenship: it was a privilege enjoyed only by a few (inherited, merited, won after long service). Many Roman citizens lived hundreds of miles from the city but still claimed the privileges of their status. St Paul, for example, born in Ephesus, claimed the right to be tried in Rome.

**codex**
a manuscript parchment; a code of laws

*Codex*, originally spelled *caudex*, first meant 'tree trunk' but eventually acquired additional meanings. For example, Juvenal used *codex* to mean 'a wooden block', to which men were tied as punishment. Terence used *codex* as a term of derision, the equivalent of 'blockhead'. Finally *codex* came to mean a book made of bound wooden slabs, with printing scratched into wax coatings on the slabs. But *codex* also has the meaning of 'a code of laws'. Two famous *codices*, plural of *codex*, are the *Codex Alexandrinus* and the *Codex Sinaiticus*, but there are many others, including the *Codex Juris Canonici*, the official collection of ecclesiastical laws of the Roman Catholic Church.

### coelum non animum mutant qui trans mare currunt
those who cross the sea change the sky, not their spirits

In this delightful sentence from Horace's *Epistles*, we are cautioned that a change of scene – here *coelum*, 'the heavens', also given as **caelum** does not change us. As we travel from one place to another, what we see with our eyes may change dramatically, but we are the same people we were when we started our journey. If we are to credit Horace, then, we cannot flee our destinies, nor by flight can we change what is fundamental to our nature: the grass is not greener on the other side of the street. Fortunately, in *Paradise Lost* Milton sends a happier message:

> The mind is its own place, and in itself
> Can make a Heav'n of Hell, a Hell of Heav'n.

### cogito ergo sum
I think, therefore I exist

One of the most famous of all philosophic axioms, known – perhaps imperfectly – by every freshman student of philosophy. Descartes, in his *Discourse on Method*, used it as the starting point for his philosophic system.

### coitus interruptus
interrupted coitus

### collegium
colleagueship

A *collegium* – in Roman times the word described the connection between a pair of colleagues as well as within a group of colleagues – can be applied now to members of any group united by common interest or pursuits: a college faculty or department, a society of scholars, an ecclesiastical group living together to pursue a common purpose, etc.

**compos mentis**
of sound mind

A person in his right mind is adjudged *compos mentis*, translated more literally as 'in full possession of mental powers', while a person not of sound mind is said to be **non compos mentis**. The two terms are used loosely today by people unqualified to make either judgement. More properly the two expressions find use in legal writing and court testimony.


**compos sui**
master of himself

*Compos sui* is a condition few of us can aspire to in this world of big government and big corporations. Unlike the poet W.E. Henley (1849–1903), we cannot declaim:

I am the master of my fate:
I am the captain of my soul.


**conditio sine qua non**
indispensable condition

When an agreement stands or falls on the inclusion of a particular condition, that condition may be called a *conditio sine qua non*, literally 'a condition without which not'. (See *causa sine qua non.*)


**confer**
compare

The abbreviation of *confer*, cf., is seen in English most often in scholarly writing. The abbreviation may be used, for example, to invite readers to compare an author's discussion with that presented in another work, but the important fact to bear in mind is that cf. does not mean merely 'see' or 'see also'. The full Latin word *confer* is never seen in modern texts.


**confiteor**
I confess

The opening word of the Catholic general confession said at the beginning of the Mass.

## Congregatio de Propaganda Fide
Congregation for the Propagation of the Faith

The committee that supervises messages and missions for the Vatican. The committee members are cardinals and other Church officials.

## coniunctis (or conjunctis) viribus
with united powers

Anyone acting in concert with others can be said to be acting *conjunctis viribus*, towards a common goal. 'The Allied Powers pledged to act *conjunctis viribus* when an attack was directed at any of the several nations.'

## consensus
agreement

This word, taken into English with the same meaning as its Latin ancestor, bedevils poor spellers of English, who fail to associate *consensus* with the English word 'consent'. Thus, we often see the misspelling 'concensus', reflecting a confusion with the word 'census'. The Latin word *census* has a meaning somewhat like that of our English 'census'. The Romans registered all citizens and their property for purposes of taxation, calling the registration a *census*. 'Consent', as one already knows, has little to do with taxation. The word 'consent' derives from *consentire*, 'to agree', whose past participle is *consensus*. While it is primarily to help poor spellers that *consensus* is given its own entry here, *consensus*, as soon will be seen, is central – forgive me – to several useful Latin expressions.

## consensus audacium
a conspiracy

Cicero used this phrase, literally 'agreement of rash (men)', to describe conspiracies by people intent on some nefarious purpose. In his time, Cicero acted as self-appointed watchdog of men in government and frequently held forth in the Senate to accuse his political enemies of conspiracy.

**consensus facit legem**
consent makes law

The principle that an agreement between two parties is binding if the agreement does not in any way violate existing law.

**consensus gentium**
widespread agreement

This phrase, literally 'unanimity of the nations', is used to describe perfect or nearly perfect agreement on some matter by everyone concerned. So a generally accepted belief or opinion may be described as a *consensus gentium*.

**consensus omnium**
agreement of all

A happy situation, in which all parties involved in a discussion of policy, procedure or the like have reached unanimity. Another form of this phrase is **consensu omnium**, with the meaning 'by general consent'. 'We acted *consensu omnium* in all decisions affecting our members' welfare.' Tacitus, in his *Annales*, made telling use of *consensu omnium* in describing an inept politician: **Omnium consensu capax imperii nisi imperasset**, 'By general consent, he would have been considered capable of governing if he had never governed.' A classic put-down.

**consilio manuque**
by stratagem and manual labour

The motto of Figaro in Beaumarchais's *Barber of Seville*. Figaro was a barber who used wit and resourcefulness in struggling against the abuses of government. *Consilio manuque* could well serve also as the motto of the unfortunate intellectual who must make his living by practising a trade because he cannot find employment more suitable to his true talent and education.

**consule Planco**
in the good old days

The literal translation of this phrase is 'in the consulship of Plancus'. Two consuls held office in Rome at any time. Their term of office under the republic was one year, but under the empire the term was reduced to a few months. Romans often referred to past years by the names of the consuls who then held office. Thus, Horace in his *Odes* referred to the carefree days of his youth as *consule Planco*. Plancus was consul in 42 BC, when Horace was twenty-three and serving on the wrong side – under Brutus – at Philippi, where Augustus and Antony defeated Brutus and Cassius. Horace returned to Italy after the defeat to find that his family's property had been confiscated, his own prospects diminished. The phrase *consule Planco* has survived in the sense of 'in the good old days'. Since, justifiably or not, most people look back upon their early years as good times, Horace has given us a handy alternative for lectures to our juniors that begin too often with 'When I was young ...' Nonetheless, recalling the experience of Plancus, we must recognize the irony in *consule Planco*. The good old days too often are good only in retrospect.


**consummatum est**
it is completed

Christ's last words on the cross, John 19:30.


**contra bonos mores**
against the best interests of society

This phrase, literally 'contrary to good morals', is used in law to describe an action or a contract considered harmful to the moral welfare of society. Thus, a contract to commit a crime, for example, is a contract *contra bonos mores* and therefore legally void. (See *pro bono publico*, a happier legal phrase.)


**contraria contrariis curantur**
opposites are cured by opposites

The principle of allopathic medicine, the traditional form of medicine, which seeks to fight disease by using remedies – antibiotics are a good example – that produce effects totally different from the effects produced by the disease under treatment. This principle is the direct opposite of that of homoeopathic medicine. (See *similia similibus curantur*.)

**coram iudice** (or **judice**)
before a judge who has jurisdiction

This phrase, literally 'in the presence of a judge', is used by lawyers to describe a hearing before a court that has the authority to act in the case.

**coram populo**
in public

This phrase, literally 'in the presence of the people', was used by Horace in his *Ars Poetica*, in suggesting that a dramatist, in deference to sensibilities of audiences, should not depict murder on stage.

**cornu copiae**
horn of plenty

*Cornu copiae* is also written in Latin as *cornucopia*. The legend of Amalthea, the nymph who nursed Zeus when he was an infant, has it that she fed the young god with goat's milk. (Another version of the story says Amalthea was a goat that suckled the young Zeus.) Zeus endowed the horn of the goat with the capability of producing whatever the owner of the horn desired. Since Amalthea was the possessor of this *cornu copiae*, she could get from it whatever she wanted. Even today the cornucopia is the symbol of abundance.

**corpus delicti**
the terrible evidence that a crime has been committed

The *corpus delicti*, literally 'the body of the crime', is the fact or set of facts needed to establish that a crime has been committed. In murder, for example, it is proof that a person has been murdered. When we hear this phrase in old Hollywood detective movies, the district attorney is usually the character who complains to the chief of police that there is no *corpus delicti*, and therefore there can be no prosecution of the heavy we all suspect. The audience squirms at the familiar complaint, believing the DA means the police cannot find the *body* of the victim, the 'corpse', but what is really meant is that the district attorney cannot prove that a crime has been committed, even though a hacked-up corpse might be a good beginning. If the crime in question is arson, to take another example, the *corpus delicti* may be proof of arson, not merely a burned-out building; if the crime is burglary, evidence that a safe has been rifled, rather than merely an empty safe.

### corpus iuris *(or* juris)
body of law

The collected laws of nation, state, or city are its *corpus iuris*. Church law is **corpus iuris canonici**, and civil law is **corpus iuris civilis**.

### corrigenda
items to be corrected

The singular form, *corrigendum*, literally 'that which is to be corrected', is ample evidence of the frailty of human beings: Because it is a singular form, it is almost never used. By contrast, the plural, *corrigenda*, is frequently found in manuscripts as well as in published books and journals. *Corrigenda* in its modern meaning calls attention to corrections that must be made here and there throughout a work before it is published (or republished).

### Cras amet qui nunquam amavit;
### Quique amavit, cras amet.
May he love tomorrow who never has loved before;
And may he who has loved, love tomorrow as well.

This couplet forms the refrain of the *Pervigilium Veneris*, 'The Night Watch of Love', written by an anonymous poet who obviously believed in love: yesterday, today and tomorrow, as well as every day before and after. Samuel Butler, in *The Way of All Flesh*, expressed the same confidence in the desirability of love: ' 'Tis better to have loved and lost than never to have loved at all.'

### credo quia absurdum est
I believe it because it is unreasonable

A justification of faith on the basis that there is no need to understand. It is the essence of faith not to seek a rational explanation in matters spiritual. This profound statement of belief is also given as **credo quia impossibile est**, 'I believe it because it is impossible.'

### cui bono?
who stands to gain?

This expression, attributed by Cicero to a Roman judge and literally meaning 'To whom for a benefit?' is mistakenly taken to mean 'What good will it do?' Rather, it must be understood to be the question raised by anyone wise in the ways of the world. A new bridge is proposed for which there is no apparent need. Which contractor wants to make a fat profit from the project? The question may be replaced by *cui bono?*

### cuius regio eius religio
the ruler of a territory chooses its religion

Historically, the religion practised by the ruler of a region determined the religion practised by his or her subjects. Today, *cuius regio eius religio*, literally 'Whose the region, his the religion', may be used in a broader sense. For example, the white shirt, striped tie and dark suit dictated for male employees of certain corporations; the spectacle of football players, under compulsion, bowing their heads in prayer before a game (and then being told to 'get out there and hit them hard').

### cum grano salis
with a grain of salt

One of the most familiar Latin expressions. When one does not fully believe something or someone, *cum grano salis* implies a certain caution or reserve. Salt was a valuable commodity in the ancient world, so a grain of salt is not to be taken as a trivial matter. It is worth noting that the English word 'salary' derives ultimately from the Latin: *salarium* was the money allotted to Roman soldiers for purchase of salt – hence, their pay.

### cum laude
with praise

A US university degree awarded *cum laude* is the third rank of honours, **magna cum laude**, 'with great praise', is second in rank, while **summa cum laude**, 'with greatest praise', is the top rank. A student who has staggered through to a degree with barely passing grades is said jocularly to be graduated **summa cum difficultate**, 'with greatest difficulty'.

## cum privilegio
with privilege

An authorized or licensed edition of a book is an edition *cum privilegio* or an **editio** ('edition') **cum privilegio**.

## cum tacent clamant
silence is an admission of guilt

This expression, literally 'When they remain silent they cry out', is from the first of Cicero's orations against Catiline, one of his political opponents. Despite the tradition of Western justice that a person accused of crime is not required to give evidence against himself the popular view is that silence is an admission of guilt. Thus *cum tacent clamant* is a powerful argument outside a court of law (and sometimes inside a jury room).

## curae leves loquuntur ingentes stupent
minor losses can be talked away, profound ones strike us dumb

This maxim of Seneca's, from his play *Phaedra* is more literally translated as 'Slight griefs talk, great ones are speechless'. Seneca's observation may be tested at a wake, when conversation of the most inane sort occupies many of the people present, yet others speak not at all.

## currente calamo
with pen running on

Anything written without care or forethought can be described as having been written *currente calamo*. A writer who never stops to reflect need not take his pen from the page.

## curriculum vitae
a résumé

This term, literally 'the course of (one's) life', is used to denote the written account of qualifications submitted to support a job application. In Britain, the term is commonly used by applicants in all fields. In America, résumé is more common among business applicants while *curriculum vitae* is preferred by academics eager to avoid association with the world of commerce. Because *curriculum vitae* is a mouthful, it is often referred to as a *cv*.

**custos morum**
a censor

*Custos* means 'guardian' or 'watchman'. Thus, a **custos incorruptissimus** is 'a young man's guardian', since such a person can be trusted never to stray in any way; he is superlatively incorruptible. *Mores* means 'morals', so *custos morum* is 'the guardian of morals' and a Latin term for 'censor'.

### dabit deus his quoque finem
God will grant an end even to these (troubles)

This saying from Virgil's *Aeneid* counsels hope, even in the darkest hour. (For a similarly optimistic observation from Virgil, see *forsan et haec olim meminisse iuvabit.*)

### dabit qui dedit
he who has given will give

A suitable maxim for the professional fund-raiser. Those who once have contributed to a worthwhile cause can be counted upon to reach down deep again. It is for this reason that those of us who give even once to charity – or who buy once by mail order – soon find ourselves inundated with requests that we do so once again and again and again.

### damnant quod non intelligunt
they condemn what they do not understand

The perennial cry of the obscure poet or struggling avant-gardist.

### damnum absque iniuria (or injuria)
no basis for a lawsuit

This legal term, literally 'loss without harm', refers to loss of property or violation of a right without possibility of legal redress. Not exactly the sort of thing on which lawyers thrive.

**de asini umbra disceptare**
'little things affect little minds'

This Latin phrase, freely rendered above in a line quoted from Disraeli's novel *Sybil*, may be translated literally as 'to argue about the shadow of an ass'. The phrase finds ready use in derogating the work of a lesser scholar who spends a lifetime explicating the unimportant, as well as in hushing the disputatious bore ever ready to quibble over the trivial.

**de bono et malo**
come what may

The literal translation of this phrase is 'of good and bad'. When one has decided to forge ahead come what may, for better or for worse, the decision is made *de bono et malo*.

**deceptio visus**
an optical illusion

Literally 'a deception of vision'.

**de die in diem**
continuously

Literally 'from day to day' and also given as **diem ex die**, with the same meaning. 'Those of us who are happily employed work *de die in diem*, never looking up from our work until we finish the task in hand.' An apt rendering of either of the Latin phrases would be 'day in, day out'.

**de duobus malis, minus est semper eligendum**
choose the lesser of two evils

Recognizing the realities facing those who must often choose between less than perfect alternatives, Thomas à Kempis, the fifteenth-century theologian, adjures us in this Latin phrase to make the best of a bad situation, saying literally, 'Of two evils, the lesser is always to be chosen.'

**de facto**
in reality

This common expression is literally translated as 'from the fact'. It differentiates that which exists in fact (*de facto*) from that which exists legally (*de iure* or *de jure*). Thus *de facto* rulers, in contrast with *de iure* rulers, wield power even though no legal process has been employed in establishing their power.

**de gustibus non est disputandum**
there's no accounting for tastes

This widely used expression, literally 'About tastes there is no disputing', wisely tells us that taste is a personal matter. Since no amount of persuasion can succeed in changing a person's taste – and rightfully so – it is better not to argue about matters of personal preference. In time, a person's taste may change, but not because of anything others may say. This saying is sometimes given as **de gustibus et coloribus** ('and colours') **non disputandum**, more often merely as *de gustibus*, 'concerning tastes'.

**Dei gratia**
by the grace of God

Found in such expressions as **Regina Dei Gratia**, 'Queen by the Grace of God', and **Imperator Dei Gratia**, 'Emperor by the Grace of God'. The implication is that anyone functioning *Dei gratia* has direct access to the Divinity.

**de integro**
anew

Anything that commences with the past obliterated from memory begins *de integro*. (See *de novo*.)

**de iure** (or **de jure**)
sanctioned by law

See *de facto*.

**delenda est Carthago**
Carthage must be destroyed

The story behind this phrase is well worth recounting. For two centuries or so, Carthage was the only real rival to Rome in the western Mediterranean. In fact, until the two superpowers came into conflict in Sicily in 264 BC – war broke out because Rome feared Carthaginian expansionism in southern Italy – Carthage had been the dominant power. Rome prevailed in the First Punic War (264–261), but the peace terms left Carthage still strong enough to threaten Rome. Sure enough, there was a Second Punic War (218–201). This time, Hannibal's brilliant strategy nearly destroyed Rome, but Scipio Africanus, the Roman general, defeated Hannibal – perhaps at Zama, an ancient town in present-day Tunisia – in the decisive battle of that war, and Carthage was no longer a power to reckon with. Half a century later, when Carthage was still a threat to Rome, war broke out once again, in part because of the influence of Cato the Elder, who repeatedly egged the Roman Senate on with his ominous phrase *delenda est Carthago*: 'Carthage must be destroyed.' Since Carthage was not a match for Rome's military power, the outcome of this Third Punic War (149–146) was predictable. Soon enough the Carthaginians, led to believe they would be given generous peace terms, were tricked into surrendering. But once peace prevailed, the great city of Carthage was destroyed by the Romans, and a century was to pass before it was resettled and became a prosperous city once more. Cato's *delenda est Carthago* survives as an ironic reminder that a ruling clique in a powerful nation can have its way in crushing a helpless rival if it musters the rhetoric to stir irrational passions.

**delineavit**
he (or she) drew (this)

An indication, along with the artist's name, of the creator of a painting, drawing, or sculpture: *delineavit Publius* or *del. Publius*, 'drawn by Publius'.

**delirium tremens**
the DTs

Literally 'trembling delirium', *delirium tremens* is the mental disorder associated with over-indulgence in drinking. The afflicted person characteristically trembles excessively and hallucinates.

**de minimis non curat praetor**
don't bother me with petty matters

The literal translation of this expression is 'A praetor does not occupy himself with petty matters'. A praetor in ancient Rome was a magistrate who assisted the consuls by administering justice and commanding armies. In Caesar's time, there were sixteen *praetores*. Since a praetor was a busy man, we can appreciate his insistence on saving his time for important matters. Today anyone wanting to suggest that he or she is above small matters may use this phrase, inevitably with the intention of impressing others with the importance of the concerns that normally occupy an important person's time. A related expression is the legal precept **de minimis non curat lex**, 'the law does not concern itself with trifles', which is used to justify refusal by a court, particularly an appellate court, to hear a suit, on the basis that a court's time must not be taken up with matters of small import. This phrase, often abbreviated *de minimis*, explains why income tax payments that are a few pounds short of what they should be are sometimes accepted without complaint.

**de mortuis nihil nisi bonum**
speak kindly of the dead

Tradition has it that Chilon of Sparta, one of the wise men of sixth-century BC Greece, is the author of this saying, literally 'of the dead, (say) nothing but good'. (Of course, Chilon used Greek rather than Latin, so what we have here is the Latin translation.) The advice to all of us that one should speak well of the recently dead or remain silent is at least as old as Homer. *Nihil*, 'nothing', is also given as a contraction, *nil*.

**de nihilo nihil**
nothing comes from nothing

Persius, the first-century AD Roman poet, advises us in his *Satires* that effort is required to produce anything of value. He goes on to tell us that anything once produced cannot become nothing again: **in nihilum nil posse reverti**. Persius is believed to have been parodying Lucretius (first century BC), who propounded the physical theories of Epicurus (fourth century BC). As a cynical comment, *de nihilo nihil* can be distorted to denigrate a failed work as the product of a person of little talent. The implication is, 'How can we expect better from such a source?'

### de novo
anew

Like *de integro, de novo* is an expression used in describing a fresh start. 'Let's forget the past and begin *de novo*.'

### Deo favente
with God's favour

An expression used to invoke God's co-operation in ensuring success for an action about to begin or to express gratitude for the success of an activity completed successfully. '*Deo favente*, I will pass my examination.' 'I have always been able to make a good living, *Deo favente*.'

### Deo gratias
thanks to God

When an enterprise has turned out well, one may say *Deo gratias* or *Deo favente*. *Deo gratias* appears frequently in Latin prayers, but it is also used jocularly. 'As the curtain came down on the opera after five long hours, some were shouting *bravo* while others were muttering *Deo gratias*.'

### Deo iuvante (or Deo juvante)
with God's help

This expression, also given as **Deo adiuvante** or **Deo adjuvante**, has the same intent and is used in the same manner as *Deo favente*.

### de omni re scibili et quibusdam aliis
I know everything worth knowing, and more

*De omni re scibili*, literally 'of all the things one can know', was the pretentious title of a work by a fifteenth-century Italian scholar, Pico della Mirandola, who prided himself on being able to debate with anyone on any subject. In derision, someone (perhaps Voltaire) added to it *et quibusdam aliis*, literally 'and even of several other things'. The result is an elegant phrase one can use to puncture the pomposity of a self-proclaimed expert on everything under the sun.

### Deo optimo maximo
to God, the best, the greatest

Once a favourite dedication (abbreviated DOM) for a work of art. (See *domino optimo maximo*).

### Deo volente
God willing

Yet another expression (abbreviated DV) used to enlist the aid of the deity when initiating an enterprise or looking forward to the future. *'Deo volente,* we will all be here next year to celebrate our fifty-first anniversary.'

### de pilo pendet
we've reached the critical stage

This expression, literally 'it hangs by a hair', is used to describe the tense moment when a sickness, a sports event, a military action or the like appears to be in the lap of the gods. *De pilo pendet* derives from the situation in which Damocles found himself. Dionysius I, the tyrant of Syracuse, in order to demonstrate that the life of a ruler was no bed of roses, had Damocles, a fawning member of the court, seated at a royal banquet with a sword suspended over his head by a single hair. We recall Damocles in the phrase 'sword of Damocles', with the meaning 'an impending disaster', and our word 'impending' has its origin in *pendere*, the Latin word for 'to hang'.

### de profundis
out of the depths (of despair)

A cry of deepest anguish, from the opening words of Psalm 130: 'Out of the depths have I cried unto thee, O Lord.' This psalm is often read in the Catholic burial service, but *de profundis* has other associations: Oscar Wilde, after being imprisoned in 1895 for homosexual practices, wrote an essay called 'De Profundis', which was published posthumously.

**de proprio motu**
spontaneously

Literally 'of one's (or its) own motion'. 'Everything happened *de proprio motu* from then on; we played no further part in shaping events.'

**De Rerum Natura**
On the Nature of Things

A philosophic poem by Lucretius, first century BC, outlining a science of the universe based on the philosophies of Democritus and Epicurus and attempting to prove that all things in nature operate without reliance on the supernatural.

**desipere in loco**
to play the fool on occasion

Horace, in his *Odes*, wrote **dulce est desipere in loco**, literally 'Sweet it is (*dulce est*) to relax at the proper time'. Students who complete their examinations successfully and writers who finish a book on schedule, for example, know how to enjoy themselves fully, knowing their work is done. The rest of us, who spend our time in idleness when faced with pressing obligations, never know the restorative value of that great delight, earned leisure.

**deus ex machina**
an unlikely and providential intervention

*Deus ex machina*, literally 'a god out of a machine', describes an unexpected occurrence that rescues someone or something from an apparently hopeless predicament. An impoverished widow about to be evicted receives a legacy from a long-lost aunt or wins first prize in a million-pound lottery. This is the stuff that bad fiction or drama is made of, so it is no surprise that *deus ex machina* is usually applied to narrative works, especially to the work of playwrights and novelists who find themselves enmeshed in complexities of their own devising and incapable of bringing their plots to a close without relying on improbable coincidence. Thus, when the US Cavalry – in vintage Hollywood style – comes over the hill just as the long-lost brother of its commanding officer is about to be scalped, the writer has resorted to *deus ex machina*.

The expression has its origin in ancient Greek theatre, especially in certain plays of Euripides. When the complexities of plot and character appeared incapable of resolution, a god was set down on stage by a mechanical crane to sort things out and make them right. Greek gods could do anything.

### Deus misereatur
may God have mercy

The title of Psalm 67, which begins *Deus misereatur* and continues (in English) 'and bless us, and cause His countenance to shine upon us'.

### Deus vobiscum
God be with you

An appropriate saying, literally 'God with you', to use when taking one's leave. The singular form is **Deus tecum**.

### Deus vult
God wills it

Battle-cry of the First Crusade, in the final years of the eleventh century, which resulted in recovery of the Holy Land from the Muslims. The people who had gathered to hear an address by Pope Urban II at the Council of Clermont in 1095 responded *Deus vult*. Since most armies normally proceed on the basis that God favours them or orders them to fight, it is not surprising that the Crusaders used *Deus vult* as a battle-cry. The motto of the German armies during the two great wars of the twentieth century was *Gott Mitt Uns*, 'God (is) with us.'

### diem ex die
continuously

See *de die in diem*.

### diem perdidi
another day wasted

Titus, Emperor of Rome, having passed an entire day without performing a good deed, is reported to have said, *Diem perdidi,* literally 'I have lost a day'. Anyone who has a job to do that requires sustained effort in order to meet a tight deadline may use the phrase to express despair at the end of an unproductive day, another day down the tube.

### dies faustus
an auspicious day

The Romans paid a great deal of attention to omens. For example, a Roman who saw a meteor or a flight of birds would look upon the display as an indication of a *dies faustus*, literally 'a day bringing good fortune'. (*Faustus* is the perfect passive participle of *faveo*, 'favour.') **Dies infaustus** has the opposite meaning.

### Dies Irae
Days of Wrath

A thirteenth-century Latin hymn on the Day of Judgement, sung at the requiem Mass.

### dii penates
guardians of the household

*Dii penates* were the household gods of the ancient Romans, a people given to a plethora of gods. *Dii*, the plural of *deus*, 'god', is also written *dei* and *di*. *Penates* alone also means 'household gods'. However expressed, the intention is clear: Roman families and their homes were looked after by special deities. (See *lares et penates*.)

### dis aliter visum
man proposes, God disposes

A literal translation for Virgil's *dis aliter visum*, in the *Aeneid*, is 'It seemed otherwise to the gods'. An appropriate expression for rationalizing a failed effort.

### disiecta (or disjecta) membra
fragments

A phrase, literally 'scattered limbs', used to describe brief quotations from literary works. Horace wrote of *disiecta membra poetae*, 'limbs of a dismembered poet', suggesting that one can perceive the quality of good poets even in brief quotations from their works.

## disputandi pruritus ecclesiarum scabies
the theologian's urge to debate is an incurable disease

Sir Henry Wotton, 1568–1639, an English poet and diplomat, wrote this sentence, literally 'An itch for disputation is the mange of the churches', in *A Panegyric to King Charles*, and it was later used as part of Wotton's own tombstone inscription. (He is also recalled for his definition of an ambassador: 'an honest man sent to lie abroad for the good of his country'.)

## divide et impera
divide and rule

This ancient political maxim, adopted by Machiavelli, is also given as **divide ut regnes** and as **divide ut imperes**, all of which mean 'divide in order to rule'. One stratagem of a wily leader is to encourage his followers to squabble continually among themselves, making it easy for him to have his own way.

## divina natura dedit agros, ars humana aedificavit urbes
God made the country, and man made the town

A maxim, literally 'Godlike nature gave us the fields, human skill built the cities', of Marcus Terentius Varro, first-century BC Roman scholar, in *De Re Rustica*.

## Divinitatis Doctor
Doctor of Divinity

Abbreviated DD. It is worth mentioning that the Latin word *doctor* means 'teacher', not 'physician'.

## dixi
that settles the matter

This word, literally 'I have spoken', signals that 'I will say no more on the matter, and no one else may speak further.'

**docendo discimus**
we learn by teaching

A maxim well understood by inspired teachers and leading to the advice **doce ut discas**, 'Teach in order to learn'.

**doctus cum libro**
having book learning

This expression, literally 'learned with a book', describes those of us who lack practical knowledge.

**Domine, dirige nos**
Lord, direct us

Motto of London.

**Domino optimo maximo**
to the Lord God, supreme ruler of the world

This phrase, literally 'to the Lord, best and greatest', is the motto of the Benedictine Order. It is included here for the edification of those who are fond of an after-dinner glass of Benedictine and brandy. On the label of a bottle of Benedictine, a liqueur originally made by monks of the Benedictine Order, appears DOM, the abbreviation of *Domino optimo maximo*. (See *deo optimo maximo*.)

**Dominus illuminatio mea**
the Lord is my light

Motto of Oxford University.

**Dominus vobiscum**
God be with you

Another way to bid farewell. The singular form is **Dominus tecum**. (See *Deus vobiscum*.)

**donec eris felix, multos numerabis amicos**
when you're successful, everyone wants to be your friend

This observation, literally 'As long as you are fortunate, you will have many friends', from Ovid's *Tristia*, reflects bitterly on human nature. It concludes with **tempora si fuerint nubila, solus eris**, literally 'If clouds appear, you will be alone'. Even in ancient Rome, there were fair-weather friends.

## dramatis personae
cast of characters

This familiar expression, literally 'the persons of the drama', although primarily denoting the characters or actors in a play, can be taken also as the characters in a novel, poem, film etc., as well as the participants in the events of everyday life. 'The hostages and their captors constituted a familiar *dramatis personae.*'

## ducit amor patriae
love of country guides me

The motto of the patriot, literally 'Love of country guides'. (See *Dulce et decorum* ...)

## dulce est desipere in loco
sweet it is to relax at the proper time

See *Desipere in loco.*

## dulce et decorum est pro patria mori
there's no greater honour than to die for one's country

We meet these words in Horace's *Odes*, literally 'It is sweet and fitting to die for the fatherland'.

## dum spiro spero
while I breathe, I hope

## dum tacent clamant
their silence speaks volumes

The literal meaning of this saying is 'Though they are silent, they cry aloud'. Silence may have great significance, in certain situations even constituting an admission of guilt.

**dum vita est spes est**
while there's life, there's hope

**dum vivimus vivamus**
while we live, let us live

The motto of the Epicureans, followers of Epicurus, who taught that pleasure is the goal of morality but defined a life of pleasure as one of honour, prudence and justice – in short, advocating living one's life to make for tranquillity of body and mind. These teachings were corrupted later – epicureanism today is equated with self-indulgence and luxurious tastes.

**dura lex sed lex**
the law is hard, but it is the law

Just about the only thing one can say when trying to convince others to pay their income tax or to obey a law generally considered unfair or harsh.

**dux femina facti**
*cherchez la femme*

We have Virgil, in the *Aeneid*, to thank for this Latin phrase, literally 'A woman was the leader in the deed'. We must also bow in the direction of countless fictional detectives for their adoption of Dumas's advice, *cherchez la femme* if you want to get to the bottom of things.

**ecce homo**
behold the man

The Latin translation of the words Pontius Pilate (John 19) used in showing the people the bound Christ wearing the crown of thorns. *Ecce homo* is the title taken for many paintings depicting Christ in this condition.

**ecce signum**
look at the proof

This phrase, literally 'behold the sign', adjures us to examine the evidence, the proof. In *Henry IV, Part I*, Falstaff boasts of his encounter with a small army of attackers bent on his destruction: 'I am eight times thrust through the doublet, four through the hose; my buckler cut through and through; my sword hacked like a handsaw – *ecce signum!*'

**e contrario**
on the contrary

**editio cum notis variorum**
an edition with the notes of various persons

An edition of a literary text, called in English a 'variorum edition', that offers variant readings of the text as well as notes and commentary by scholars. (See *variorum*.)

**editio princeps**
first edition

Of ancient texts, the first printed edition.

**editio vulgata**
common edition

See *terra es, terram ibis.*

**e.g.**
for example

See *exempli gratia.*

**eheu fugaces labuntur anni**
alas, the fleeting years glide by

A sad line from Horace's *Odes*, reminding us – as though we need help in remembering – that Maxwell Anderson was right when he told us that our 'days dwindle down to a precious few'. *Eheu*, alas! (Turn quickly to *carpe diem.*)

**ei mihi**
alas

A frequent ejaculation of the sorely tried Aeneas of Virgil, who lacked the patience of Job.

**eiusdem** (or **ejusdem**) **farinae**
birds of a feather

This expression, literally 'of the same flour', is used to characterize people of the same nature – 'cut from the same cloth' – usually in a pejorative sense.

**e libris**
See *ex libris.*

**emeritus**
having served his time

This word has its origins in Roman military tradition, with the meaning of 'a soldier who has served his time honourably'. In modern usage, it is applied to a university officer who is rewarded for faithful service with the rank, for example, of 'emeritus professor'. The designation carries no formal obligation to the institution but usually entitles the person so designated to continue to use the facilities of the institution and to attend ceremonies as an honoured member of the academic community. Emeritus rank is the academic equivalent of the gold watch given to good old what's-his-name upon retirement. University women who retire from academic life may be given **emerita** rank, although some institutions eschew this feminine form.

**ense et aratro**
serving in war and in peace

The motto, literally 'with sword and plough', of the farmer who serves his country by putting down the plough, *aratrum*, in time of war to take up the sword, *ensis*, for his country. In time of peace, he returns to his farm to serve his country once again. The motto applies equally to any civilians who leave their peacetime jobs to take up arms for their country. Isaiah looks forward to the time when 'They shall beat their swords into ploughshares, and their spears into pruning hooks; nation shall not lift up sword against nation, neither shall they learn war any more.'

**e pluribus unum**
one out of many

Motto of the United States of America, indicating that a single nation was made by uniting many states.

**ergo**
therefore

**errare humanum est**
to err is human

The recognition, also given as **errare est humanum**, that rubbers are attached to pencils for good reason. Alexander Pope, in 'An Essay on Criticism': 'To err is human, to forgive, divine.'

**erratum**
error

An error in printing or writing is given the dignified appellation *erratum*, plural *errata*. An *errata* is a list of such errors.

**est modus in rebus**
choose the middle ground

With these words from Horace's *Satires*, literally 'There is a proper measure in things', we are advised against extremes.

**esto perpetua**
may she live forever

Said to be the dying words of Fra Paolo Sarpi (1552–1623), historian and philosopher, speaking of his native Venice.

**et al.**
abbreviation of **et alii, et aliae, et alia**

This abbreviation is used in writing to avoid a lengthy listing. **Et alii** is masculine, so it is properly used in speech to mean 'and other men' when preceded by the name of a male or to mean 'and other people'. **Et aliae** is feminine, so it is properly used in speech to mean 'and other women'. **Et alia** is neuter, so it is properly used in speech to mean 'and other things'. Educated persons do not pronounce the abbreviation *et al.* 'And others' is said for *et al.*

**et cetera**
and so on

This familiar phrase, used only when speaking of things, not people, literally means 'and the rest'. In speech, its abbreviation, **etc.**, is given the pronunciation of the full phrase.

**et hoc genus omne**
and all that sort

This expression, literally 'and everything of the kind', is used to indicate others of a class of persons or things. It finds use as a pretentious substitute for **et cetera**.

**etiam atque etiam**
again and again

**et in Arcadia ego**
I've known good times

Literally 'And I too (lived) in Arcadia': a tombstone inscription in Poussin's painting *The Arcadian Shepherds*. Arcadia, in the Greek Peloponnesus, stood for easy living, happiness, idylls.

**et nunc et semper**
from now on

Literally 'now and forever'.

**et sic de similibus**
and that goes for the others too

This phrase, literally 'and so of similar (people or things)', is used to suggest that whatever has been said of one person or topic under discussion holds true for related matters as well. (See *ab uno disce omnes*.)

**et tu, Brute**
so you're mixed up in this too

According to tradition, reflected in Shakespeare's *Julius Caesar*, the final words of Caesar, falling before the conspirators' knives:

'*Et tu, Brute!*' [literally "You also, Brutus"] Then fall Caesar.' The line, memorized by all schoolchildren, reflects Plutarch's account of the death of Caesar. Caesar resisted his attackers until he realized that Brutus, his trusted ally, had joined them. Blessed with this provenance, *Et tu, Brute* has become the classic recognition of betrayal by a trusted friend.

**et ux.**
and wife

The lawyer's abbreviation for **et uxor**: 'John Smith *et ux.*' 'And wife' is said for *et ux.*

**ex aequo et bono**
equitably

A principled person does everything *ex aequo et bono*, literally 'according to what is just and good'.

**ex animo**
sincerely

A person who speaks from the bottom of his heart speaks *ex animo*, literally 'from the heart'.

**ex cathedra**
with authority

When a pope speaks *ex cathedra*, literally 'from the chair', he is considered to speak infallibly, and the chair he speaks from is the papal throne. Thus, when experts speak authoritatively on matters in their fields of knowledge, we may say that they speak *ex cathedra* or that they have made *ex cathedra* statements. We may also apply *ex cathedra* ironically to dogmatic pronouncements by the pretentious self-proclaimed expert. It must be pointed out that before the *cathedra* was the pope's chair – indeed, before there were popes – it was the chair of a teacher.

**excelsior**
ever upward

**exceptio probat regulam**
the exception establishes the rule

This proverb, shortened from the legal maxim **exceptio probat regulam in casibus non exceptis** ('in the cases not excepted'), is mistakenly taken as 'The exception proves the rule', leading the unwary to think that any self-respecting rule must have an exception. What is meant is that the existence of an exception to a rule provides an opportunity to test the validity of a rule. Finding an exception to a rule enables us to define the rule more precisely, confirming its applicability to those items truly covered by the rule.

**excudit**
made by

A printer or engraver's mark, literally 'he (or she) struck (this)', used to identify the person who executed the work. The abbreviation for *excudit* is **excud**.

**exeat**
permission to be absent

An *exeat*, literally 'let him (or her) go forth', is an official permission granted to a priest to leave a diocese or monastery. In British universities, an *exeat* is permission granted for temporary absence from a college.

**exegi monumentum aere perennius**
I have raised a monument more durable than bronze

Horace started his final ode with these words, suggesting that his *Odes* would bring him immortality. Only the likes of a Horace should apply this sentence to their own work.

**exempli gratia**
for instance

This expression, literally 'for the sake of example', is always abbreviated **e.g.** in English. It is used correctly to introduce an example, incorrectly to mean 'that is'. (See *id est*.)


**exeunt**
they leave the stage

We are accustomed to seeing *exeunt*, literally 'they go out', as a stage direction in old plays, with the meaning 'two or more actors leave the stage'. When *exeunt* is followed by **omnes**, the playwright is telling us that all the actors on stage at the time are to leave. The singular of *exeunt* is the familiar **exit**, a stage direction meaning 'he (or she) leaves the stage'.


**exit**
See *exeunt*.


**exitus acta probat**
the end justifies the means

Literally 'the result validates the deeds'. This proverb avers that any means – no matter how foul – may be used if the intended result is a good one. But take care.


**ex libris**
from the library of

This familiar legend, also given as **e libris**, translated literally as 'from the books', commonly appears on book plates. The phrase is followed by the owner's name.


**ex mero motu**
spontaneously

Literally 'out of pure, simple impulse'. 'He insisted that no one had exerted pressure on him, that he acted *ex mero motu*.'

**ex more**
according to custom

**ex nihilo nihil fit**
nothing comes from nothing

Lucretius, the first-century Roman poet, wrote in *De Rerum Natura* of the creation of the world: **Nil posse creari de nilo**, 'Nothing can be created out of nothing', which is also rendered as *ex nihilo nihil fit*, suggesting that every effect must have a cause. Lucretius agreed with the fifth-century BC Greek philosophers who theorized that the world could not have been made from nothing. They thought it had been created from the accidental joining of atoms falling from space. The Latin **atomus** means 'atom' or – remember that this theory antedated quarks and mesons by more than two millennia – 'that which is indivisible'. But there is ambiguity in *ex nihilo nihil fit* and in its English translation. Thus the Latin phrase is applied rather broadly today, and *ex nihilo nihil fit* may be used to suggest that a dull mind cannot be expected to produce great thoughts, anything worth doing requires hard work, you can't get blood from a stone, and the like. (See *de nihilo nihil.*)

**ex officio**
by virtue of an office

Officers of an institution usually serve on many of its committees not because they have personal qualifications needed on the committees but because they hold certain offices. Thus the chief executive officer of a corporation usually is a member *ex officio* of all the important committees of the corporation.

**ex parte**
from one side only

A legal expression, literally 'from a party', applied to a proceeding in which only one side of the case is presented, and the opposing side is absent. Naturally, there is the presumption of partisan testimony in an *ex parte* proceeding.

### ex pede Herculem
from a sample we can judge the whole

This expression, literally 'From the foot, a Hercules', means we can extrapolate accurately when we know a single pertinent fact. The phrase is an allusion to Pythagoras, the sixth-century BC Greek mathematician and philosopher who calculated the height of Hercules by measuring and comparing the length of many Greek stadiums. Since Hercules' stadium at Olympia was longest by far, Pythagoras deduced that Hercules' foot was longer than the foot of lesser men (or gods). Knowing that a man's height is proportional to the length of his foot, Pythagoras was able to establish a credible height (the whole) for Hercules from the length of his foot (the sample). Inspector Maigret, Sherlock Holmes, Hercule Poirot and Nero Wolfe may owe a great deal to Pythagoras. (See *ex ungue leonem*.)

### experto credite
trust me

In the absence of evidence to the contrary, we are adjured by Virgil, in the *Aeneid*, literally to 'Believe one who has experience'. The fragility of this advice is implicit in its use: *Experto credite* is too often cited by the person who may understand little and have even less evidence to offer but has spent a long time practising his trade. 'That stock is a good buy, *experto credite*,' said the broker.

### ex post facto
from what is done afterward

We are all experts *ex post facto*, who can always give the correct answers to all problems once we know how things have worked out. An *ex post facto* law, normally not permitted in British constitutional law, is one that can be applied retroactively; even though such a law is passed after a particular case has been settled, it would be deemed applicable even to previously closed cases.

### ex proprio motu
voluntarily

Anyone who acts entirely without encouragement or coercion does so *ex proprio motu*, literally 'of one's own accord'.

**ex tempore**
extemporaneously

Anyone speaking *ex tempore*, Cicero's phrase, does so 'without preparation'. The phrase can also be used in the sense of 'without premeditation'.

**extinctus amabitur idem**
how quickly we forget

A marvellously insightful observation from the *Epistles* of Horace, with the literal meaning 'The same man will be loved after he's dead.' Horace understood how quickly a person's bad reputation is forgotten once he's safely underground, and we have ample evidence of the aptness of *extinctus amabitur idem* in the work of revisionist biographers and historians.

**ex ungue leonem**
from a sample we can judge the whole

Another way of saying that we can tell the whole from a single part, with the literal meaning 'From a claw, the lion'. (See *ex pede Herculem*.)

**ex uno disce omnes**
from one example you may deduce the rest

This maxim, literally 'From one, learn of all', advises us to generalize from one example, a precept that must be applied intelligently. *Ex uno disce omnes* may be useful for certain cases – if one oak leaf turns brown, they all will; if one quart of milk in a batch is sour, the entire batch will not be potable; if one war is hell, all wars will be hell – but if one child ... others may not.

## fabas indulcet fames
hunger makes everything taste good

Literally 'Hunger sweetens beans' – beans, of course, being the poor man's fare. *Fabas indulcet fames* is another way of saying *fames optimum condimentum*, 'Hunger is the best seasoning'.


## facile princeps
number one

A felicitous phrase, literally 'easily first', used to designate the acknowledged leader in any field.


## facilis descensus Averno
the descent to hell is easy

Avernus, a lake in Campania, was considered by the Romans to be an entrance to hell. *Avernus*, literally 'without a bird', is said to have been so named because poisonous vapours arose from it and were said to draw birds down into its waters, where they perished. Thus, *facilis descensus Averno*, a line from Virgil's *Aeneid*, cautions us that it is easy to fall but, once fallen, difficult to make one's way back up. Beware that first false step!


## facta non verba
actions speak louder than words

*Facta non verba*, literally 'Deeds, not words', holds that protestations of good intentions count for little. Action is what we need.

**fama semper vivat**
may his (or her) good name live forever

A useful expression when invoking the name of an illustrious or revered person. 'This good woman, *fama semper vivat*, saw fit to remember us in a bequest that will help our cause for many years to come.' (Notice the difference in the translation of *fama* in the next entry. In Latin, as in any other language, words acquire additional meanings through use.)

**fama volat**
rumour travels fast

In the *Aeneid*, Virgil tells us that nothing travels faster than scandal: **Fama malum quo non aliud velocius ullum**. *Fama volat*, another phrase from the *Aeneid*, provides a handier way to convey the same thought.

**fames optimum condimentum**
Hunger is the best seasoning

See *fabas indulcet fames*.

**Fata obstant**
the gods willed otherwise

The *Fata* were the three Roman goddesses of fate or destiny: Nona, Decuma and Morta. Any human action that went amiss was blamed on the opposition of the *Fata*, 'The Fates'. So Virgil's phrase in the *Aeneid*, *fata obstant*, literally 'The Fates oppose', could be cited. Similarly, anything that concluded happily was ascribed to the co-operation of the *Fata*. Thus the Romans had a foolproof device for refusing to take action or for turning down a request. *Fata obstant* beats 'My hands were tied.'

**Fata viam invenient**
the gods will find a way

Another saying (see the preceding entry) from Virgil's *Aeneid*, literally 'The Fates will find a way', but this time an expression of optimism. Yet it is worth noting that the Romans here reveal once again their inclination to leave things in the lap of the gods.

Modern man is more apt to say: 'God helps those who help themselves.' The Romans had more fun.

### favete linguis
hold your tongue

This expression from Horace's *Odes*, with the literal meaning 'favour with your tongues', is a warning to utter no words of bad omen during a religious rite: 'Say nothing lest what you say hurt another or bring down on us an unfavourable act of the gods.' The Latin for telling someone to keep silent under ordinary circumstances is **quin taces**.

### fecit
made by

*Fecit*, literally 'he or she made (it)', was an artist's way of signing a work. *Fecit* is followed by the artist's name. (See *excudit*.)

### felicitas habet multos amicos
prosperity has many friends

When things are going well for us, we never lack for friends. When our fortunes turn …

### felix qui nihil debet
happy is he who owes nothing

### felix qui potuit rerum cognoscere causas
fortunate is he who has been able to learn the causes of things

This line from Virgil's *Georgics* praises those of superior intelligence who can grasp the secrets of nature and so raise themselves above reliance on superstition.

### festina lente
make haste slowly

Suetonius, in *Divus Augustus*, attributes this bit of wisdom to the Emperor Augustus, who moved cautiously, step by step, to transform Rome from a republic to an empire ruled virtually by one man. Thus, what appears to be salutary advice may have Machiavellian overtones.

### fiat iustitia (or justitia) ruat caelum
let justice be done though the heavens fall

The unyielding precept that the law must be followed precisely, regardless of the circumstances and eventualities.

### fiat lux
let there be light

The Latin version of one of the opening verses of Genesis.

### fiat voluntas Tua
Thy will be done

Familiar words from the Latin version of the Lord's Prayer, from Matthew's Gospel.

### fide et amore
by faith and love

### fide et fiducia
by faith and confidence

### Fidei Defensor
Defender of the Faith

*Fidei Defensor*, abbreviated FD, is one of the many titles of British monarchs. Henry VIII was awarded the title by Pope Leo X. Ironically the king rebelled against the Church a few years later.

### fides Punica
a double cross

This expression, literally 'Punic faith', refers to the Carthaginians – the Latin name *Punicus* means 'Phoenician', and it was the Phoenicians who founded Carthage. The Punic Wars resulted in the destruction of Carthage by the Romans. The distrust of the

Carthaginians by the Romans was exemplified in *fides Punica* – the Romans intended the same meaning when they soke of **ars Punica**, 'the Punic art', **fraus Punica**, 'Punic deceit', and **perfidia Punica**, 'Punic treachery'. (See *delunda est Carthago* for an illustration of the trustworthiness of Rome.)

### fidus Achates
bosom pal

In the *Aeneid*, Virgil characterized Achates, companion of Aeneas, as *fidus Achates*, literally 'faithful Achates', giving us a convenient Latin substitute for 'best friend'.

### finem respice
look to the end

Appropriate advice for anyone about to take an irreversible step or launch a risky venture.

### finis coronat opus
the end crowns the work

Easily understood by anyone who has completed a major project and rejoiced in its completion.

### floruit
he [she] flourished

*Floruit*, often abbreviated fl., is used to date the period of a person's prime, particularly when exact birth and death dates are unknown: 'Somadeva (*fl.* 11th century) was a Sanskrit author.'

### fluctuat nec mergitur
unsinkable

*Fluctuat nec mergitur*, literally 'It is tossed by the waves but does not sink', is the motto of Paris, which has a ship as its emblem. Like any other city that has existed for a long time, Paris has had its ups and downs. In ancient times, for example, it was called *Lutetia*, from the Latin word *lutum*, meaning 'mud', reflecting the fact that the City of Lights was then only an aggregation of mud hovels. Anyone for Paris in the spring?

**fons et origo**
the source and origin

**forsan et haec olim meminisse iuvabit**
Perhaps this will be a pleasure to look back on one day

Virgil, in the *Aeneid*, knowing that time cures all (see *temporis ars medicina fere est*), gives us this formula for surviving difficult times by looking ahead to what surely will be happier days.

**fortes fortuna iuvat** (or **juvat**)
fortune helps the brave

A proverb of Terence, in *Phormio*, given by others as **fortuna favet fortibus**, 'Fortune favours the brave'. We make our own luck.

**fortiter in re, suaviter in modo**
resolutely in action, gently in manner

A characterization of the estimable person who does unhesitatingly what must be done but accomplishes the deed as inoffensively as possible. An excellent motto for personnel managers.

**fortuna favet fortibus**
fortune favours the brave

See *fortes fortuna iuvat.*

**fronti nulla fides**
never judge a book by its cover

This advice from Juvenal's *Satires*, more literally 'No reliance can be placed on appearance', warns us against hasty judgements of character made solely on what the eyes perceive.

**fugaces labuntur anni**
you wake up one morning and find you are old

Literally 'The fleeting years glide by'. (See the next two entries and *eheu fugaces labuntur anni*.)

**fugit hora**
time flies

Persius, a first-century AD Roman poet, used this expression, literally 'The hour flies', to tell us that it's later than we think.

**fugit irreparabile tempus**
we cannot stop time in its tracks

*Tempus fugit*, an expression we employ to mean 'time flies', is taken from *fugit irreparabile tempus* – itself a slightly shortened form of a line from Virgil's *Georgics* – with the literal meaning 'Time irretrievably is flying'. (See *eheu fugaces labuntur anni*.)

**fuit Ilium**
Troy has had it

Virgil, declaring that Troy – called Ilium by the Romans – no longer existed, wrote *fuit Ilium*, literally 'Troy has been', but better rendered as 'Troy is no more'. We now know a great deal about the riches of Troy, thanks to the work of Heinrich Schliemann, the gifted amateur archaeologist, so the lesson we learn from *fuit Ilium* is that if such a gem can fall, the rest of civilization had better watch out. What Virgil implied in *fuit Ilium* was 'and now Rome is number one' – that is, from a world destroyed, a new world is created. But now that the Roman Empire is gone ...

**furor**
madness

*Furor* combines with other Latin words to give us some useful phrases: **furor loquendi**, 'a rage for speaking', **furor poeticus**, 'poetic frenzy', and **furor scribendi**, 'a rage for writing'.

## gaudeamus igitur
let us therefore rejoice

The opening words of a student song of German origin, sung sometimes at academic exercises. Even without knowing what the words mean, anyone who looks back fondly at undergraduate life – proving that absence makes the heart grow fonder – will automatically choke up on hearing this song. After all, the words following are **iuvenes** (or **juvenes**) **dum sumus**, meaning 'while we are young'. (See **eheu fugaces labuntur anni** for a bit of irony.) But to put college life in perspective, it is worthwhile to know that the English word 'gaudeamus' (or 'gaudy') means a revel by undergraduates, who traditionally imbibe spirits and otherwise carouse to celebrate successful completion of their examinations. Those of us who are unfamiliar with the melody of *gaudeamus igitur* may hear it in Brahms' *Academic Festival Overture*.

## genius loci
the guardian spirit of a place

The Romans believed that everybody born into this world was assigned a *genius*, a guardian spirit that accompanied that person from then on, determining the character and fortunes of the person until death – and beyond. The Romans also believed that every house and every institution had the same arrangement, a *genius loci*. The modern use of this term is intended to be taken as 'the character of a place', for example, the *genius loci* of one's *alma mater*.

## genus irritabile vatum
the irritable race of poets

Horace used this phrase in his *Epistles*, giving us a way to chide testy men of letters. The usual word for 'poet' is **poeta**. In replacing *poeta* with a form of **vates**, which means 'a prophet or seer who makes divine utterances', Horace – later poets also applied *vates* to members of their profession – was using a more honorific term but one that conveys a vaguely sinister sense.

### Gesta Romanorum
*Deeds of the Romans*

Title of a medieval collection of stories in Latin, with each story intended to teach a moral lesson.

### Gloria in Excelsis Deo
Glory be to God on high

The first words of the familiar hymn, from Luke's Gospel.

### Gradus ad Parnassum
a step to Parnassus

The title of a dictionary of prosody much used by past generations of British schoolboys learning to write Latin verse. A *gradus*, as any work of its type is known, supplies the length of syllables in spoken Latin as well as suggesting poetic phraseology. Parnassus, a mountain in Greece, has two summits, one of which was consecrated to the Muses by the ancient Greeks. For this reason Parnassus is thought of as the seat of poetry.

### grammatici certant
grammarians dispute

The beginning of a line from Horace's *Ars Poetica*, concluding **et adhuc sub iudice** (or **judice**) **lis est**, thus giving us: 'Grammarians discuss, and the case is still before the courts.' *Grammatici certant*, by itself, can be used to characterize any problem that is still to be resolved by the experts, in particular disagreement among critics over the quality of a work of art.

### gratias tibi ago
thank you

## habeas corpus
you may have the body

A 'habeas corpus' is a legal writ, a feature of British and United States law that protects an individual against arbitrary imprisonment by requiring that any person arrested be brought before a court for formal charge. When the writ is executed, the court hears the complaint under which the person has been detained and rules on the validity of the arrest. If the charge is considered valid, the person must submit to trial; if not, the person goes free. So when a lawyer threatens, 'I'll slap a habeas corpus on you so fast, it'll make your head swim', full protection of the law is being sought for the accused.

## haec olim meminisse iuvabit (or juvabit)
time heals all wounds

See *forsan et haec olim meminisse iuvabit.*

## Hannibal ad portas
the Russians are coming

This expression, literally 'Hannibal is at the gates', was used to alert the citizens of Rome to imminent danger. Hannibal, the commanding general of Carthaginian armies during the Second Punic War, was so feared by the Romans that *Hannibal ad portas* became a proverbial expression, in use well after Hannibal and his armies no longer were a threat and carrying the meaning 'Our country's in danger'. Comparable warnings – e.g. 'a threat to national security' – are not unknown today. (See *delenda est Carthago.*)

**haud ignota loquor**
you know as well as I that …

A rhetorical expression, literally 'I speak of things by no means unknown', implying that an audience understands – and agrees with – a speaker's interpretation of some aspect of the subject under discussion, thus giving the speaker licence to gloss over the putative merits of the point being made.

**hic et nunc**
here and now

A person who demands immediate action, such as repayment of a debt, would say he wants it *hic et nunc*.

**hic et ubique**
here and everywhere

**hic iacet** (or **jacet**)
here lies

The opening words of many an old tombstone inscription.

**hinc illae lacrimae**
so that's what's eating you!

In the play *Andria*, Terence used this phrase, literally 'hence those tears', to mean 'So that is the true offence, the underlying reason for the annoyance.' The rare modern father who finally grasps the reason for a child's display of moodiness might say, '*Hinc illae lacrimae*, you want to spend all your weekends with your mother.'

**hoc age**
get at it!

Literally 'Do this' but used to adjure people to apply themselves to their work.

**hoc anno**
in this year

**hoc erat in votis**
this is what I once longed for

These words from Horace's *Satires*, more literally 'This was what I wished', introduce a listing of things he once wanted. The sense is that passage of time has altered his desires, so we use this phrase when looking back at our abandoned dreams.

**hoc est vivere bis vita posse priore frui**
to live twice is to make useful profit from one's past

This epigram by Marcus Valerius Martialis (*c.* AD 100), known today as Martial, may be interpreted in a variety of ways, all of them positive. Experience is the best teacher. Plan ahead. Don't look back, but capitalize on what you have been through. Who would dispute the efficacy of any of these?

**hoc genus omne**
all this sort

A phrase from Horace's *Satires* that can be applied to people with the meaning 'all people of that type', as well as in broader senses: 'I quickly tire of discussions of home computers, word processors and *hoc genus omne.*'

**hoc loco**
in this place

**hoc opus, hic labor est**
this is the tough part

Virgil, in the *Aeneid*, tells in this phrase, literally 'This is work, this is labour', that once we go wrong we shall find it difficult to get back on the right track. Virgil was referring to how easy it is to fall into Avernus, the lower depths, and then how hard to make one's way back. (See *facilis descensus Averno*). But we can use his phrase aptly to prescribe behaviour for many difficult situations we encounter in life on earth.

**hoc volo, sic iubeo (or jubeo), sit pro ratione voluntas**
the fact that I wish it is reason enough for doing it

This statement from Juvenal's *Satires* translates more literally as 'This I will, thus I command; let my will serve as reason'. Excellent text for a sampler destined for hanging at home or in the office of an editor or business executive.


**hodie mihi, cras tibi**
my turn today, yours tomorrow

These words, literally 'Today to me, tomorrow to you', reflect the inevitability of change, so they are used in old epitaphs to remind viewers of their own mortality.


**homo doctus in se semper divitias habet**
a learned man always has wealth within himself


**homo homini lupus**
'man's inhumanity to man'

The bitter translation quoted above from Robert Burns has persisted in our culture with the same meaning as *homo homini lupus*, literally 'Man is a wolf to man', an observation adapted from the play *Asinaria*, by Plautus, and appropriate whenever one reads a newspaper.


**honoris causa**
honorary

An academic degree granted *honoris causa*, literally 'for the sake of honour', is bestowed as recognition of merit without formal examination. As we know well, degrees awarded *honoris causa* too often are rewards for financial generosity: **pecuniae causa**, 'for the sake of wealth'. (For another point of view, see *pecunia non olet*.)


**hora fugit**
the hour flies

One of several Latin expressions reminding us that life passes all too quickly.

**horas non numero nisi serenas**
I do not count the hours unless they are bright

A favourite inscription for sundials.


**horresco referens**
I shudder to relate

In Virgil's *Aeneid*, Aeneas says these words as he recounts the death of Laocoön, a priest of Apollo. Laocoön saw that his sons were being attacked by serpents sent by Apollo or Athena. Good father that he was, Laocoön went to his children's defence and was killed along with them, supposedly for his role in attempting to dissuade the Trojans from accepting the horse the Greeks used to penetrate Troy. The only good thing about *horresco referens* is that it gives us a welcome relief from 'You wouldn't believe it', 'I kid you not' and 'too horrible for words'.


**horribile dictu**
horrible to relate

In describing a particularly bloody automobile accident, for example, one might interject *horribile dictu* just before launching into the most shocking details of the narrative. (See *mirabile dictu*.)


**hostis humani generis**
enemy of the human race

Few qualify for this appellation, suitable in our time for the likes of Adolf Hitler.


**humanum est errare**
To err is human

See *errare humanum est*.

**iacta** (or **jacta**) **alea est**
the die is cast

See *alea iacta est*.


**ianuis** *(or* **januis***)* **clausis**
behind closed doors

Any private meeting can be called a meeting *ianuis clausis*, literally 'with closed doors', the most celebrated examples being the meetings held by the college of cardinals in the Sistine Chapel to elect a pope.


**ibid.**
See next entry


**ibidem**
in the same place

A weapon in the arsenal of scholarly terms. Abbreviated **Ibid.** in a footnote, and often italicized (underscored in manuscript) because it is Latin, *Ibid.* makes reference to an identical source cited in an immediately preceding footnote. For example, in the footnote '[16] *Ibid.*, p. 77,' the source referred to in footnote 15 is being referred to again, but this time citing page 77 of that source. Small wonder the young scholar complains: 'Half my life is spent writing *Ibid.*, *op. cit.* and *loc. cit.*'

**idem**
the same

Sometimes abbreviated **id.**, this scholarly term appears in footnotes containing more than one reference to works by the same author. It is used in place of the author's name after the initial reference.

**id est**
that is

This scholarly term, abbreviated **i.e.**, is used in identical fashion as its English translation: to clarify a statement just made. The abbreviation *i.e.* is heard more and more in the speech of those who do not know the Latin phrase – nor even the meaning of the term – so misuse is almost as common as correct use. The most frequent mistake reflects confusion of *i.e.* with **e.g.**, the abbreviation of *exempli gratia*, 'for example'. Perhaps we are better advised to use the English equivalents in place of these abbreviations.

**id genus omne**
all that sort

Used in the same way as *hoc genus omne*.

**i.e.**
See *id est*.

**Iesus** (or **Jesus**) **Nazarenus Rex Iudaeorum** (or **Judaeorum**)
Jesus of Nazareth, King of the Jews

Abbreviated INRI

**ignis aurum probat, miseria fortes viros**
life is not a bowl of cherries

Senece, in *De Providentia*, warns us that there will be trouble in our lives and we must learn to come to grips with it, telling us literally: 'Fire tests gold; adversity (tests) strong men.' (Seneca apparently knew something of the differential melting points of metals.)

## ignis fatuus
will-o'-the-wisp

*Ignis fatuus*, literally 'foolish fire', signifying any misleading or deluding goal, is so called for the phosphorescent light sometimes seen at night above marshy ground and thought to be caused by the combustion of methane rising from decaying vegetable matter. Anyone who attempts to follow such light is misled, hence the meaning 'will-o'-the-wisp'.

## ignorantia legis neminem excusat
ignorance of the law excuses no one

Also given as **ignorantia iuris** (or **juris**) **non excusat**, 'Ignorance of the law does not excuse.' An even broader expression is **ignorantia non excusat**, 'Ignorance does not excuse', which goes beyond the realm of law, enabling us to upbraid an unfortunate who says, 'But I didn't know ...'

## ignoti nulla cupido
we don't want what we can't see

Ovid's thought in *Ars Amatoria*, literally 'no desire (exists) for a thing unknown', is excellent for young parents to keep in mind if they want to preclude unreasonable requests from their children.

## imo pectore
See *ab imo pectore*.

## in absentia
in (one's) absence

One may be awarded a university degree *in absentia* or convicted of a crime *in absentia*, in the former case because of inability to appear for the academic ceremony, in the latter because one is beyond the reach of the law.

**in aeternum**
forever

**in articulo mortis**
at the point of death

A statement made *in articulo mortis*, literally 'in the grasp of death', carries special weight in law, since it is believed that a person about to die has nothing to gain, perhaps much to lose, from lying.

**in bello parvis momentis magni casus intercedunt**
in war great events are the results of small causes

Anyone who has participated in war can confirm this observation, made by Caesar in his *Bellum Gallicum*. Battles are usually won by the armies that blunder least. Applied more broadly, Caesar's words tell us to pay attention to detail in any enterprise.

**in camera**
in private

Literally 'in a chamber' and applied especially to a hearing held by a judge in chambers or in a courtroom with public and Press excluded.

**in cauda venenum**
watch out for the part you can't see

The Romans knew that the scorpion's sting was in its tail, so *in cauda venenum*, literally 'In the tail is the poison', warns us to look beyond the obvious in judging potential danger. Thus, a speech that starts out innocuously may gather spite as it proceeds and climax in a malicious peroration: *in cauda venenum*.

**incidis in Scyllam cupiens vitare Charybdim**
out of the frying pan into the fire

Scylla was a nymph who was changed into a sea monster, in Homer's *Odyssey* said to inhabit a rock in the Strait of Messina – it separates Italy from Sicily – opposite the whirlpool that was the home of Charybdis, another sea monster. Scylla and Charybdis may be thought of as our modern devil and deep blue sea, as sailors careful to avoid one threat usually ended up being caught by the other: *Incidis in Scyllam cupiens vitare Charybdim*, literally 'You fall into Scylla in trying to avoid Charybdis.' The message is clear: although life usually demands that you face problems to attain any reasonable goal, exercise due caution lest you be blind-sided. In short, don't jump from the frying pan into the fire.

**incipit**
here begins

The first word in many medieval manuscripts.

**Index Librorum Prohibitorum**
List of Prohibited Books

A list published by Church authorities naming books currently out of bounds for most Catholics.

**in dubio**
in doubt

**in esse**
in being

Used to contrast things actually existing with those **in posse**, literally 'in potentiality'.

**in extenso**
word for word

An unabridged text is given *in extenso*, literally 'in full'.

**in extremis**
at the point of death

This unhappy phrase, also given as *in articulo mortis*, designates the final moments of a person's life.

**in flagrante delicto**
red-handed

When someone is caught in the act of committing a crime, he has been caught *in flagrante delicto*, literally 'while the crime is blazing'. (The phrase is also applied to situations involving lesser embarrassments.) Our own 'red-handed' is almost as vivid, if the hands are thought of as being covered with blood.

**infra**
below

A scholarly term used to call the reader's attention to something that follows in a text. It is usually preceded by **vide** ('see'). The oppositive of **vide infra**, 'see below', is **vide supra**, 'see above'.

**infra dignitatem**
undignified

This phrase, literally 'beneath (one's) dignity', is used to indicate that a suggested or contemplated act does not befit one's character or standing. The phrase is shortened to *infra dig.* by those in the know.

**in futuro**
in the future

**in hoc signo vinces**
in this sign thou shalt conquer

Emperor Constantine, on his way to battle, is said to have seen a cross appear in the sky, carrying these words. He had the message painted on his standard and went on to victory.

**in limine**
on the threshold

Used to describe something that is about to happen or beginning to happen.

**in loco parentis**
in the place of a parent

Anyone who serves *in loco parentis* may be considered to have responsibilities of guardianship, either formal or informal, over minors.

**in medias res**
into the thick of it

Authors who eschew slow beginnings for their stories, but plunge right into the action, put their readers *in medias res*, literally 'into the middle of things'.

**in medio tutissimus ibis**
you shall go safest in the middle course

Ovid counselling conservatism in *Metamorphoses* and providing the prevailing political wisdom for politicians.

**in memoriam**
to the memory of

This expression, literally 'in memory', is widely used in inscriptions, epitaphs etc.

**in naturalibus**
stark naked

Literally 'in a state of nature'.

**in nomine Patris et Filii et Spiritus Sancti**
in the name of the Father and of the Son and of the Holy Spirit

**in omnia paratus**
ready for anything

This phrase, literally 'prepared for all things', echoes *semper paratus*.

**in ovo**
immature

This expression, literally 'in the egg', can be used to characterize anything that is still in an undeveloped state. 'Modern education too often leaves its beneficiaries just as it found them, *in ovo.*'

**in pace, ut sapiens, aptarit idonea bello**
in peace, like a wise man, he appropriately prepares for war

The advice of Horace in his *Satires*, used by modern advocates of a strong war machine as the best strategy for guaranteeing peace, even though it has been followed for centuries and has yet to produce lasting peace. (See *qui desiderat pacem praeparet bellum.*)

**in partibus infidelium**
in the lands of the infidels

This phrase, usually abbreviated *in partibus*, is used in English as part of an ecclesiastical title. For example, 'bishop *in partibus*' designates a bishop who bears the title of the office but has no religious jurisdiction, since he serves in an area under religious control of another group.

**in pectore**
in secret

Anything done *in pectore* is done literally 'in the breast', such as designation of a cardinal by a pope without public announcement. The designation is said to be *in pectore.*

**in perpetuum**
forever

Also given as **in perpetuo.**

**in pleno**
in full

Payment *in pleno* is payment in full.

**in posse**
potentially

See *in esse*.

**in praesenti**
at present

*In praesenti* means now rather than *in futuro*.

**in re**
regarding

This phrase, literally 'in the matter of', is used in legal documents and notices.

**in rerum natura**
in the nature of things

**in saecula saeculorum**
forever and ever

Anything that has continued for a very long time can be said to have existed *in saecula saeculorum*, literally 'for ages of ages'.

**insalutato hospite**
without saluting one's host

This phrase refers to taking one's leave in a great hurry – for example, leaving a party without saying proper goodbyes. It also may be interpreted as 'taking French leave', an old expression for leaving without announcement – for example, skipping town without paying one's debts. The French call this doubtful practice *filer à l'anglaise*, 'to take English leave', an instance of the not-too-infrequent linguistic phenomenon of ascribing doubtful practices to the members of cultures other than one's own.

**insanus omnis furere credit ceteros**
every madman thinks everybody else is mad

Syrus gave us this penetrating observation in his *Maxims*. Who among us can see their own faults? The thief accuses everybody else of dishonesty; the adulterer says we are all unfaithful.

**in se**
in itself

See *per se*.


**in situ**
in its natural location

*In situ*, literally 'in place', is an expression used by scholars, who may say, for example, that an observation or experiment was performed *in situ*, signifying that it was made in the natural or original location of the material or process under study. 'A field examination of the archaeological find was performed *in situ* before the shards were removed.' The opposite of *in situ* would be **in vitro**, literally 'in glass' – think of a test tube, for example – and indicating a laboratory, hence artificial, setting to which the material or process has been moved. 'A great deal is heard these days about *in vitro* fertilization.' A third expression, **in vivo**, literally 'in that which is alive', is encountered in the writings of scientists. It describes experiments performed in or on a living organism.


**instar omnium**
worth all of them

*Instar omnium* is the expression Cicero used in speaking of Plato, to indicate that one Plato is worth all other men combined. The rest of us should be cautious in characterizing anyone as *instar omnium*.


**in statu quo**
in the same state

*In statu quo*, literally 'in the state in which', is used to refer to the condition of something at a particular time – for example, **in statu quo ante bellum**, 'in the same state as before the war', and **in statu quo ante**, 'in the same state of things before they were changed'. (See *status*.)

**integer vitae**
blameless of life

These are the opening words of a beautiful sentence in Horace's
*Odes*: **Integer vitae scelerisque purus non eget mauris iaculis
neque arcu**, with the meaning 'An upright man, free of guilt, needs
no weapon to defend himself'. The initial words, *integer vitae*, may
be used alone to describe a person who lives an honourable life.

**intelligenti pauca**
a word to the wise

This useful phrase, literally 'to the intelligent, few words', is also
expressed as **verbum sapienti**, 'A word is enough for a wise man',
implying that the unwise will not heed even a lengthy, explicit
warning.

**in tempore opportuno**
at the opportune time

**inter alia**
among other things

'His views on women's rights and nuclear disarmament *inter alia*
finally turned me against him.'

**inter alios**
among other persons

**inter nos**
between or among ourselves

The Latin equivalent of *entre nous*.

**inter pares**
between or among equals

A discussion *inter pares* is one in which the participants consider
one another peers.

**inter pocula**
over drinks

Literally 'between cups'. 'Why don't we discuss this *inter pocula?*'


**interregnum**
a period between rulers

Now an English word used to indicate a period in which there is no ruling authority. In the days of the Roman republic, it meant the time during the absence of the consuls or the time between the retirement or the death of the consuls and the election of their successors.


**inter se**
between or among themselves


**inter vivos**
between living persons

This legal phrase is used to designate a gift that is given by one living person to another, taking effect during their lifetimes.


**in toto**
entirely

*In toto* can also be translated as 'on the whole', 'altogether', 'in all' and 'completely'.


**intra muros**
within the walls

In ancient times, sturdy walls built on the perimeters of cities protected their inhabitants against invasion, and the day-to-day life of the city was conducted *intra muros*.

**in transitu**
on the way

*In transitu* has its English counterpart in the phrase 'in transit'.

**intra vires**
within the powers

A matter that is *intra vires* is within the legal power or authority of an institution or individual, as opposed to one that is **ultra vires**, beyond the legal powers.

**in utrumque paratus**
ready, come what may

Regardless of the possible outcome for any human endeavour – success or defeat, life or death – the wise person is *in utrumque paratus*, Virgil's phrase in the *Aeneid*, with the literal meaning 'prepared for either alternative'.

**in vacuo**
isolated

Physicists may study phenomena *in vacuo*, literally 'in a vacuum', but the rest of us use the term in an extended meaning – just as we use the phrase 'in a vacuum' – to indicate complete absence of communication with others, or separation from reality.

**in vino veritas**
wine loosens the tongue

There are sleeping drunks and fighting drunks and quiet drunks and talkative drunks. *In vino veritas*, an old Roman proverb, with the literal meaning 'in wine the truth', tells us that people under the influence of wine or other spirits will say things they ordinarily try to conceal.

**invita Minerva**
uninspired

Minerva, the Roman goddess of wisdom and patroness of all the arts, is obviously someone to have on your team at all times if you work in the arts. If she deserts you on a given day, your work will suffer, but you can put the blame on her by saying *invita Minerva*, literally 'Minerva being unwilling'. The phrase may also be used by critics to characterize an artist or a work of art lacking inspiration.

## in vitro
See *in situ*.

## in vivo
See *in situ*.

## ipsa quidem pretium virtus sibi
virtue is its own reward

A saying of Claudian, a late classical, fourth-century Roman who has been called the last of the Roman poets.

## ipse dixit
an unsupported assertion

This phrase, literally 'He himself said so', labels a statement as authoritative only to the extent that the reputation of its author merits trust, with the implication that there is no other guarantee of its validity: 'All we have is his *ipse dixit*.' When Cicero used this phrase, he was referring to Pythagoras, and when Pythagoras is the *ipse* in *ipse dixit*, the authority cannot be questioned.

## ipsissima verba
verbatim

Literally 'the very words'. 'Did she say that?' 'Yes, that is what she said, *ipsissima verba*.'

## ipso facto
by that very fact

*Ipso facto* has the meaning of 'absolutely, regardless of all other considerations of right and wrong'. 'By ordering troops into the presidential palace, the general was *ipso facto* guilty of treason.'

**ira furor brevis est**
anger is brief madness

Horace uses these words in his *Epistles* to tell us that anger is a momentary departure from rationality, and goes on to caution control over our passions lest they control us.


**ite, missa est**
go, the Mass is ended

The celebrant of the Mass concludes with these words, literally 'Go, it has been sent on its way.'


**ius** (*or* **jus**) **est ars boni et aequi**
law is the art of the good and the just

An elegant characterization of the law, that much maligned profession. Contrast *ius est ars boni et aequi* with the characterization offered by Mr Bumble in *Oliver Twist*: 'The law is a ass, a idiot.'


**ius** (or **jus**) **primae noctis**
*droit du seigneur*

A feudal lord had the right, literally 'right of the first night', to share the bed of his vassal's bride on her wedding night. This custom, not always practised, one must believe, gave way to requiring payment of a sum of money to the lord in lieu of exercise of *ius primae noctis*.


**iustitia** (or **justitia**) **omnibus**
justice for all

**jacta alea est**
See *alea iacta est.*

**januis clausis**
See *ianuis clausis.*

**Jesus Nazarenus Rex Judaeorum**
See *Iesus Nazarenus Rex Iudaeorum.*

**jus est ars boni et aequi**
See *ius est ars boni et aequi.*

**jus primae noctis**
See *ius primae noctis.*

**justitia omnibus**
See *iustitia omnibus.*

**laborare est orare**
to work is to pray

Motto of the Benedictine monks.


**labor omnia vincit**
work conquers all things

The phrase is a shortened form – with the tense of the verb changed from *vicit* (perfect) to *vincit* (present) – of Virgil's statement in his *Georgics*: **labor omnia vicit improbus**: 'Never-ending work conquered all things.' Virgil was describing the harshness of life following the Golden Age, when the earth had yielded its fruits without labour. Jupiter then decided to change everything, making life hard so that men would learn and become independent.


**lacrima Christi**
the tear of Christ

This mournful expression is often given as **lacrimae** ('tears') **Christi** and as **Lachryma Christi**. In the latter spelling, we see the triumph of commercialism, Lachryma Christi being a sweet wine produced in Italy.


**lapsus calami**
a slip of the pen

An error made through carelessness in writing is a *lapsus calami*. A *calamus* was a reed that found use as a pen.

## lapsus linguae
a slip of the tongue


## lapsus memoriae
a lapse of memory


## lares et penates
Roman gods of the household

The *lares et penates* looked after the safety and well-being of the home. The *lares* were usually deified heroes or ancestors; the *penates* were the gods of the storeroom, with the special duty of keeping the house free of danger. Images of these gods were kept in a shrine in every home, and offerings were made to them on family occasions. Today, the phrase 'lares and penates' has the meaning of 'household effects and personal possessions'.


## laudator temporis acti
a praiser of time past

Horace's expression in *Ars Poetica* for the bore who looks back always on the good old days, telling us that present times have nothing to recommend them. Revisionists of this stripe are always with us. Today's *laudatores temporis acti* recall the good times we all enjoyed during the Great Depression; what will be said fifty years from now about the Glorious Eighties?


## laudem virtutis necessitati damus
we give to necessity the praise of virtue

Marcus Fabius Quintilianus, known as Quintilian, was a Roman rhetorician of the first century AD. In this marvellous saying, he recognized that people give themselves the courage to face adversity by finding some benefit in it. Chaucer spoke of making 'vertue of necessitee', and Shakespeare followed with 'There is no virtue like necessity'. Without the ability to face our troubles this way, many more of us might founder.

**laus Deo**
praise (be) to God

**lex loci**
the law of the place

The Latin equivalent of 'the law of the land'.

**lex non scripta**
the unwritten law

*Lex non scripta* refers to what we call common law, the body of law derived in the English tradition from precedent without the formality of statutes and regulations, but nonetheless binding. *Lex scripta*, it follows logically, is the body of written, or statutory, law.

**lex salica**
Salic law

*Lex salica* is the law of the ancient Salian Franks, a people who inhabited a region in the Rhine valley near the North Sea. *Lex salica* became part of the French legal tradition, and the aspect of Salian law that became particularly well known is that forbidding the inheritance of an estate by female members of a family. It was because of an interpretation of this law that the French monarchy never had women as rulers.

**lex scripta**
See *lex non scripta*.

**lex talionis**
an eye for an eye, a tooth for a tooth

*Lex talionis*, literally 'the law of retaliation', is the practice of punishment in kind, dating back at least to the Old Testament, yet much in vogue today in some societies.

**licentia vatum**
poetic licence

Literally 'the licence of poets'. (See *genus irritabile vatum.*)


**licet**
it is allowed

*Licet* is the formal expression used in granting permission. 'May I be relieved of my academic responsibilities during the coming term?' '*Licet.*' (Or '*Non licet.*')


**ligonem ligonem vocat**
he (or she) calls a spade a spade

A *ligo* is really a hoe, but the phrase is construed as a compliment regardless of the tool employed. Many of us prefer people who are outspoken even to the point of rudeness, compared with pussyfooters who never let us know where they stand.


**lis sub iudice** (or **judice**)
a case not yet decided

A matter before the courts that has not yet been disposed of is a *lis sub iudice*, literally 'a lawsuit before the judge'. (See *adhuc sub iudice lis est.*)


**litterae humaniores**
the humanities

The Latin phrase, literally 'the more humane letters (or learning)', designating the Greek and Latin classics, grammar, poetry and rhetoric – all considered polite learning conducive to culture, contrasted with **litterae divinae**, theology.


**Litterarum Doctor**
Doctor of Letters

An honorary degree, abbreviated Litt.D.

**loco citato**
in the place cited

This phrase is a tool of the scholar. Abbreviated *loc. cit.*, it is used in footnotes to refer the reader to a passage previously cited: 'Morrison, *loc. cit.*'

**locum tenens**
a substitute or deputy

*Locum tenens*, literally 'one holding the place', refers to someone who is filling in temporarily for another person. The expression is said most often of physicians and clergymen.

**locus classicus**
the most authoritative or most frequently cited passage

A *locus classicus*, literally 'a classical source', is a passage commonly cited to explain or illustrate a subject.

**locus delicti**
the scene of the crime

A *corpus delicti* establishes that a crime has been committed. A *locus delicti* is the place where the crime occurred. Now all we need is the perpetrator.

**locus in quo**
the place in question

A *locus in quo*, literally 'the place in which', refers to a place where something of interest has occurred or, in a book, where a passage under discussion may be found.

**locus poenitentiae**
a place or opportunity for repentance

A legal expression denoting the period within which a person may withdraw from an assumed obligation before it becomes binding.

**locus sigilli**
the place of the seal

The *locus sigilli*, abbreviated l.s., is the place on a document for affixing the seal of the notary public or other official.

**loquitur**
he or she speaks

A stage direction, abbreviated *loq*.

**lucri causa**
for the sake of gain

Anything done in hope of financial reward or profit is done *lucri causa*. Before leaving the subject of money, it is worthwhile to cite Juvenal, in his *Satires*: **Lucri bonus est odor**, 'Sweet is the smell of money', and the line concludes **ex re qualibet**, 'obtained from any source'.

**lucus a non lucendo**
a paradoxical or absurd etymology

*Lucus* means 'a dark grove' but is said to be derived from the verb *luceo* to shine.

**lupus est homo homini**
man is a wolf to man

Plautus, in his *Asinaria*, recognized man's inhumanity to man in this phrase, suggesting that pride and avarice are the cause of lupine behaviour in humans. The wolf epitomizes predatory behaviour, of course, but we must regretfully take note that while wolves are not known to attack one another, human beings too often do.

**lusus naturae**
a freak

Literally 'a sport of nature'.

**macte virtute**
well done!

This phrase, literally 'be increased in merit', gives us a Latin equivalent for 'bravo' or 'hooray'. *Macte virtute*, like its English counterparts, commends and encourages.


**magis mutus quam piscis**
silent as the grave

Literally 'quieter than a fish'.


**magister artis ingeniique largitor venter**
necessity is the mother of invention

The Roman satirist Aulus Persius Flaccus, known as Persius, gave us this maxim, literally 'The belly is the teacher of art and the bestower of genius.'


**Magister Artium**
Master of Arts

The intermediate university degree, abbreviated MA or AM.


**magister dixit**
the master has spoken

Medieval scholastics used this phrase as an irrefutable argument, invoking Aristotle.

**magister ludi**
schoolteacher

Literally 'master of public games (in honour of the gods)'. A **ludus litterarius** was an elementary school. Modern readers know *Magister Ludi* as the title of a novel by Hermann Hesse.

**magna cum laude**
with great praise

Second honours in an American university degree. (See *cum laude*.)

**magna est veritas et praevalet**
great is truth, and it prevails

A proverb from Esdras, also given with **praevalebit** ('will prevail') as the final word.

**magnificat**
it magnifies

The Virgin Mary's response to the Annunciation (Luke's Gospel): 'My soul doth magnify the Lord', begins in Latin: **Magnificat anima mea Dominum**. Any song of praise may be called a *magnificat*.

**magni nominis umbra**
an unworthy descendant of an illustrious family

Literally 'the shadow of a great name', an unfortunate appellation for anyone who struggles unsuccessfully to emulate the achievements of senior members of his family. The expression is from Lucan's *Pharsalia*.

**magnum bonum**
a great good

**magnum opus**
one's crowning achievement

An artist's or writer's masterpiece may be called his *magnum opus*, literally 'a great work'.

**maior** (or **major**) **e longinquo reverentia**
no man is a hero to his valet

Literally 'greater reverence from afar', *maior e longinquo reverentia* calls attention to our inclination to fail to observe faults when we consider people or things from a distance – distance lends enchantment – and our inclination to find fault with everyone and everything close at hand. And, conversely, familiarity breeds contempt – faults are exaggerated when we observe them often, as in someone we love.


**mala fide**
in bad faith

Anything done *mala fide*, as opposed to **bona fide**, is done fraudulently.


**mala in se**
inherently bad

Literally 'bad in themselves'.


**malesuada fames**
hunger that leads to crime

In a description of Hell in the *Aeneid*, Virgil tells us that outside Hell's doors live Grief, Suffering, Disease, Age, Fear, Hunger and Want. Hunger (*fames*) is described as *malesuada*, literally 'persuading to evil'. A sobering thought for those who make social policy.


**malis avibus**
under unfavourable signs

The Roman propensity for employing soothsayers when planning an important move is nowhere better illustrated than in this phrase, literally 'with bad birds'. The birds referred to are birds of divination, and since they are *malae*, the omens are bad. **Avibus bonis**, literally 'with good birds', means 'under favourable signs'. Roman soothsayers often based their predictions and advice on their observations of birds, particularly birds in flight.

**malo animo**
with evil intent

The legal phrase 'with malice aforethought' is based on the Latin *malo animo*.

**malum in se**
inherently bad

Literally 'bad in itself'. (See *mala in se*.)

**mandamus**
we command

A writ of *mandamus* is an order of a higher court directing a lower court to enforce performance of a legal duty.

**manibus pedibusque**
with all one's might

Literally 'with the hands and feet'. This colourful expression reminds one of the expression 'jumping in with both feet'.

**manu propria**
with one's own hand

Anything done without assistance is accomplished *manu propria*. Medieval artists who affixed this legend to a work were telling the world they had done their work without help from apprentices.

**mare clausum**
a closed sea

This phrase describes a body of navigable water entirely within the jurisdiction of a nation, therefore closed to foreign shipping.

**mare liberum**
an open sea

*Mare liberum* is a body of navigable water open to ships of all nations.

**mare nostrum**
the Mediterranean

The Romans referred to the Mediterranean as *mare nostrum*, literally 'our sea'.

**margaritas ante porcos**
pearls before swine

Matthew's Gospel cautions against offering the uncultured anything of quality: 'Give not that which is holy to dogs; neither cast ye your pearls before swine.'

**mater dolorosa**
sorrowful mother

Any mother who has lost her child is a *mater dolorosa*, but the term is applied particularly to the Virgin Mary, mourning the death of her son.

**materfamilias**
matriarch

This term can be used to describe the mistress of a household or a matron. The meaning 'matriarch' is more appropriate for **materfamilias** because the Latin word **familia** is usually applied to an extended family. (See *paterfamilias*.)

**materia medica**
substances used as medicine

*Materia medica*, literally 'medical material', comprise the drugs and other substances physicians prescribe to cure illness. The term is also used to mean 'pharmacology'.

**mea culpa**
I am to blame

This phrase, literally 'through or by my fault', is heard in the confessional and in certain Christian prayers. **Mea maxima culpa** literally means 'through or by my very great fault'.

**medice, cura te ipsum**
physician, heal thyself

Excellent advice from Luke's Gospel for those who give advice they themselves should heed.


**Medicinae Doctor**
Doctor of Medicine

The familiar university degree, abbreviated MD.


**medio tutissimus ibis**
avoid extremes

This proverb from Ovid's *Metamorphoses* translates literally as 'You will go safest in the middle', typically Roman advice and the conventional political wisdom for those who aspire to high office. (See *in medio tutissimus ibis*.)


**me iudice** (or **judice**)
in my opinion


**membrum virile**
the male member

A euphemism for *penis*. The Latin word *penis* also means 'tail'


**memento, homo, quia pulvis es et in pulverem revertis**
remember, man, that dust thou art, and to dust shalt thou return

A Latin rendering of words in Genesis spoken by God to Adam. They are repeated on Ash Wednesday each year by priests marking the foreheads of the faithful. (See *terra es, terram ibis*.)


**memento mori**
remember that you must die

A grim reminder, literally 'remember to die', telling all of us that we must be prepared for death. A *memento mori* is a human skull or any other object serving as a reminder of the inevitability of death. It's later than you think.

**memoriter**
by rote

Literally 'by or from memory'. When we learn something *memoriter*, we learn it by heart.


**mendacem memorem esse oportet**
liars should have good memories

This saying of Quintilian, literally 'It is fitting that a liar should be a man of good memory', recognizes a difficulty the inveterate liar faces every day of his life, that of keeping his fabrications consistent. 'Oh, what a tangled web we weave ...'


**mens sana in corpore sano**
a sound mind in a sound body

Juvenal, in his *Satires*, suggests to us that we must pray for attainment of *mens sana in corpore sano*, and his phrase has found use for many centuries as the stated educational goal of many schools: to train the body as well as the mind.


**miles gloriosus**
*A Boastful Soldier*

Title of a comedy by Plautus.


**minima de malis**
the lesser of two evils

A proverb, literally 'of evils, the least', to bear in mind when we are forced to choose between less than desirable alternatives.


**mirabile dictu**
wonderful to relate

The phrase to use when one wishes to express astonishment while recounting an event of overwhelming significance or accomplishment or irony. 'Then, as the child watched, the figure, *mirabile dictu*, rose high in the air and vanished.'

**mirabile visu**
wonderful to behold

A companion phrase for *mirabile dictu*. 'There before me, **mirabile visu**, stood Bethlehem itself. My dream had been fulfilled.'

**mirabilia**
wonders

**misericordia**
mercy

The classic plea.

**Missa solemnis**
High Mass

Literally 'solemn Mass'.

**mobile perpetuum**
something perpetually in motion

The impossible dream of the inventor who rejects the laws of thermodynamics.

**mobile vulgus**
the fickle crowd

A phrase, literally 'the movable public', that recognizes the inconstancy of popular taste and the ease with which adroit politicians can influence the great mass of voters – and can lose the support of the same voters when circumstances turn against them. It is interesting to note that the English word 'mob' is a contraction of *mobile vulgus*.

**modus operandi**
manner of working

Every devotee of crime stories knows this phrase and the police abbreviation for it, MO, designating the pattern a criminal typically follows in pursuing his felonious ways. But *modus operandi* is not restricted to police use. Any work plan or scheme for doing a job may be termed a *modus operandi*.

## modus vivendi
a way of getting along together

When partners in any human enterprise must somehow manage to get along with one another despite the fact that they are not on the best of terms, they reach an accommodation, a *modus vivendi*, literally 'a way of living', which makes possible the continuing relationship.

## morituri te salutamus
we who are about to die salute you

See *Ave Caesar, morituri te salutant*.

## mors tua, vita mea
you must die so that I may live

One who can preserve his own life only by taking the life of another – think of the hired assassin or the desperately ill patient awaiting an organ transplant from a dying donor – may employ this dismal expression, literally 'Your death, my life'.

## mortis causa
in prospect of death

A legal expression, literally 'because of death', used to describe a decision made in anticipation of one's death. The phrase is seen in old wills.

## mortui non mordent
dead men carry no tales

In its literal meaning, 'Dead men don't bite', an especially colourful expression.

## mox nox in rem
let's get on with it

For anyone who believes that things are moving too slowly, an excellent call to action, akin to 'Let's get this show on the road', but literally 'Soon night, to the business'.

**multi sunt vocati, pauci vero electi**
many are called, but few are chosen

Words from Matthew's Gospel.


**multum in parvo**
much in little

A useful phrase for praising a message or a reference book that conveys much information in few words.


**mundus vult decipi**
there's a sucker born every minute

*Mundus vult decipi*, literally 'The world wants to be deceived', concludes **et decipiatur**, 'and let it be deceived'. This thought shows that twentieth-century man did not invent cynicism or opportunism.


**mutatis mutandis**
after making the necessary changes

This phrase can be rendered as 'When what must be changed has been changed' or translated more literally as 'Things having been changed that had to be changed', in the sense 'with alterations to fit the new circumstances'. Thus we may write a sentence such as: 'The new regulations governing our men's athletic teams are to apply as well to our women's teams, *mutatis mutandis.*'


**mutato nomine**
with the name changed

Literally 'the name having been changed'. This phrase becomes more interesting when we add the rest of Horace's line from his *Satires*: **de te fabula narratur**. Now we have 'With the name changed, the story applies to you.' Can you see the opportunities *mutato nomine* offers?

**nam et ipsa scientia potestas est**
knowledge is power

Francis Bacon's much-repeated and often-borrowed aphorism, literally 'For knowledge too is itself power'.


**nascentes morimur**
every day we die a little

This sobering thought from Manilius, in *Astronomica*, translates literally as 'From the moment of birth we begin to die'. It concludes **finisque ab origine pendet**, 'and the end hangs from the beginning'.


**naturam expelles furca tamen usque recurret**
the leopard cannot change its spots

This proverb from Horace's *Epistles*, literally 'You may drive nature out with a pitchfork, but it will still return', states the nature side of the nature *v* nurture debate.


**natura non facit saltum**
nature makes no leaps

This aphorism suggests the continuity and consistency of natural phenomena. Great changes that become evident as time goes by are achieved slowly and gradually, and always in consonance with underlying natural principles. Alexander Pope, in *An Essay on Man*: 'Order is heaven's first law.'

**ne Aesopum quidem trivit**
he doesn't know anything about anything

Aesop's *Fables* were used as a primer for Roman schoolboys, so *ne Aesopum quidem trivit*, literally 'He has not even thumbed through Aesop', is strong condemnation.

**ne cede malis**
do not yield to misfortunes

**nec pluribus impar**
a match for anyone

The motto, literally 'not unequal to most', of Louis XIV of France, who used the sun as his emblem and was known as *le roi soleil*, 'the sun king'. 'Not unequal to most' and its Latin counterpart are good examples of litotes, understatement in which an affirmative thought is expressed by stating the negative of the contrary thought.

**nefasti dies**
legal holidays

Certain days in the Roman religious calendar were *nefasti dies*, days in which official business of any kind was proscribed.

**nemine contradicente**
unanimously

Literally 'no one contradicting'.

**nemine dissentiente**
unanimously

Literally 'no one dissenting'.

**nemo liber est qui corpori servit**
no one is free who is a slave to his body

Seneca's observation may have been intended for those who indulged in the unbridled pursuit of pleasure (and other excesses) but it can just as easily be applied to frenzied dieters, dogged joggers, natural-food faddists and those who enrich manufacturers of vitamins.

### nemo malus felix
there is no peace for the wicked

Isaiah provides this observation, literally 'no bad man is happy'.

### nemo me impune lacessit
no one provokes me with impunity

Motto of the kings of Scotland.

### nemo repente fuit turpissimus
no one ever became extremely wicked suddenly

Juvenal, in his *Satires*, telling us we can always find a history of mischief in anyone who goes wrong in a big way.

### ne plus ultra
perfection

*Ne plus ultra* may be translated formally as 'the acme' or 'the highest attainable point', literally as 'not more beyond'. The literal sense of the phrase enables it to be used as a term expressing prohibition, in the sense of 'No further may you go', but its primary use remains that of indicating the supremacy of a product, a literary work, a system and the like.

### ne quid nimis
nothing in excess

Yet another Roman expression advocating the middle ground in all things.

### ne supra crepidam sutor iudicaret (or judicaret)
cobbler, stick to your last

These wise words, literally 'The cobbler should not judge above the sandal', of Pliny the Elder, first-century AD Roman naturalist and writer, advise us not to make judgements in areas in which we have no special competence. The story behind the expression concerns a cobbler's encounter with Apelles, a Greek painter, fourth century BC. The cobbler correctly criticized the representation of a sandal in a painting Apelles was working on. Unfortunately, he went on to criticize the way in which the subject's legs were being painted. This was too much for Apelles, who responded with his memorable rebuke: *ne supra crepidam sutor iudicaret* (also given as *sutor, ne supra crepidam*).

## nigro notanda lapillo
marking (a day) with a black pebble

In ancient Rome, a sad day or an unlucky day was marked with a black pebble, **niger lapillus**, a happy or lucky day with a white pebble, **albus lapillus**. (See *albo lapillo notare diem*.) Black pebbles were also used at Roman trials to signify a guilty verdict, white stones acquittal.

## nihil agendo homines male agere discunt
the devil finds mischief for idle hands

Literally 'By doing nothing, men learn to act wickedly'.

## nihil obstat
nothing stands in its way

*Nihil obstat* – the complete expression is **nihil obstat quominus imprimatur**, 'Nothing hinders it from being published' – are the words used by a Roman Catholic censor to indicate that a book has been found to contain nothing morally offensive or contrary to the faith. A *nihil obstat*, therefore, is a clean bill of health.

## nil admirari
to wonder at nothing

According to Horace's *Epistles*, *nil admirari*, which also translates as 'to admire nothing', may be the only way a person can become happy and remain happy. Stolid indifference is strange counsel, but is not *nil admirari* the slogan of the truly cool?

## nil carborundum

Army ranks slang 'Latin' – 'Don't let the bastards grind you down' – possibly based on 'nil desperandum'. The term is now so well known people believe it is real Latin.

## nil desperandum
never say die

As expressed by Horace in his *Odes*, meaning literally 'Nothing is to be despaired of'.

## Nil habet infelix paupertas durius in se, Quam quod ridiculos homines facit.
Nothing in poverty so ill is borne
As its exposing men to grinning scorn

The translation of two lines from Juvenal's *Satires* is by John Oldham, 1653–83, sometimes called the English Juvenal. The thought is as apt today – uncaring politicians take note – as it was in ancient Rome.

## nil nisi bonum
nothing unless good

See *de mortuis nihil nisi bonum*.

## nil novi sub sole
nothing new under the sun

This well-known phrase from Ecclesiastes reads fully: 'That which hath been is that which shall be, and that which hath been done is that which shall be done; and there is nothing new under the sun.'

## nolens, volens
whether willing or not

Literally 'being unwilling, willing'. Anyone who does something he really does not want to do does it *nolens, volens*. The phrase is used also to mean 'willy-nilly', in the sense of 'haphazardly'.

## noli me tangere
touch me not

John's Gospel has it that Christ said these words when he was approached by Mary Magdalene after the Resurrection. Today, a picture representing this scene is called a *noli me tangere*, and the impatiens plant is also called by this name, as well as by the name 'touch-me-not'.

## non bis in idem
not twice for the same thing

The Latin expression proscribing double jeopardy in the courts. Also a boy's defence against further punishment by his father after being punished by his mother.

## non compos mentis
not of sound mind

The legal expression used for any form of mental unsoundness. (See *compos mentis*.)

## non erat his locus
that was inappropriate

Literally 'That was not the place for these things'.

## non est tanti
it's no big deal

Literally 'It is not of such great importance'.

## non est vivere sed valere vita est
life is more than just being alive

From Martial's *Epigrams*, literally 'Life is not being alive but being well'. A suitable motto for those who value physical fitness. (But see *nemo liber est qui corpori servit*.)

## non ignara mali, miseris succurrere disco
I've been there myself

One rationale for helping people in distress, from Virgil's *Aeneid*. Dido, Queen of Carthage, greets Aeneas and his companions, who

are in exile: **non ignara mali**, 'No stranger to misfortune myself',
**miseris succurrere disco**, 'I learn to relieve the sufferings of others'.

**non licet omnibus adire Corinthum**
circumstances deny us certain pleasures

From Horace's *Epistles*, literally 'Not everyone is permitted to go
to Corinth'. Why? Corinth was the Paris of its day, but its
pleasures were too costly for many people. The expression is also
given as **non cuivis homini contingit adire Corinthum**, 'It does not
fall to every man's lot to go to Corinth'.

**non mihi, non tibi, sed nobis**
not for you, not for me, but for us

**non nova sed nove**
not new things but in a new way

**non obstante**
notwithstanding

**non omnia possumus omnes**
we cannot all do everything

Virgil, in the *Aeneid*, gives us this way to acknowledge a fact of
life. No one can reasonably be expected to become expert in all
things.

**non omnis moriar**
I shall not wholly die

This was Horace's way, in the *Odes*, of telling the world that his
works would live forever. Not a bad call.

**non placet**
nay

A formal way of indicating dissent, literally translated as 'It does
not please'.

**non possumus**
no way!

The answer, literally 'We cannot', given by Peter and John when they were asked to stop preaching, and now used by a pope to reject a suggested innovation in doctrine. *Non possumus* may be used by the rest of us in pleading inability to honour a request.

**non semper ea sunt quae videntur**
things are not always what they appear to be

Phaedrus, first-century AD Roman fabulist, came up with this gem to warn the unwary. In *HMS Pinafore*, William S. Gilbert put it this way: 'Things are seldom what they seem, Skim milk masquerades as cream.'

**non semper erit aestas**
be prepared for hard times

Literally 'It will not always be summer'. A similar bit of advice, this one from Seneca, is **non semper Saturnalia erunt**, literally 'The Saturnalia will not last forever', more freely 'Every day is not a holiday'. The Saturnalia, one of the principal festivals of the Romans, was celebrated in December. A time for merrymaking – often debauchery – the period saw suspension of all public business. Schools and courts were shut down, criminals were not punished, and even slaves enjoyed a taste of liberty. But the implication of Seneca's words and of *non semper erit aestas* is not lost on us: the day of reckoning will come.

**non sequitur**
it does not follow

A familiar way of indicating a logical fallacy. A conclusion offered cannot justly be inferred from the premises.

**non sum qualis eram**
I'm a different person today

Horace gave us this line in his *Odes*, literally translated as 'I am not the sort of person I was', and we may use it whenever there is a need to explain why our character and behaviour have changed.

The full line from Horace is **non sum qualis eram bonae sub regno Cinarae**, literally 'I am not what I was under the reign of good Cynara'. The poet is pleading with Venus, the goddess of love, to stop tempting him with love, since he is no longer the man he once was. It is worthwhile to recall Cynara now for reasons that soon will become clear. In the poem 'Cynara', the nineteenth-century poet Ernest Dowson used as a refrain 'I have been faithful to thee, Cynara, in my fashion' – (recall the song from *Kiss Me, Kate*) and in one of the stanzas wrote: 'I have forgot much, Cynara! gone with the wind …' Need one say more?


**non teneas aurum totum quod splendet ut aurum**
all that glitters is not gold

Literally 'Do not take as gold everything that shines like gold'. In *The Merchant of Venice*, Shakespeare gave the line as 'All that glisters is not gold'.


**nosce te ipsum**
know thyself

Plutarch attributed this advice to Plato, but a score of candidates may claim original authorship. Plutarch reported that *nosce te ipsum* was inscribed – in Greek, of course – at the oracle at Delphi.


**nota bene**
take notice

The familiar way of calling attention to something of importance in a letter or other document one is writing, and abbreviated NB. The literal meaning is 'Note well'.


**notatu dignum**
worthy of note


**novissima verba**
final words

Latin for a person's last utterance.

**novus homo**
a Johnny-come-lately

Literally 'a new man' but used to describe a *parvenu*. In the days of
the Roman republic, a *novus homo* was the first man in a family to
hold a consulship, thus ennobling both himself and his family.


**novus ordo seclorum**
a new order of the ages (is created)

Motto on the great seal of the United States. (See *annuit coeptis*
and any $1 bill.)


**nudum pactum**
an invalid agreement

Literally 'a nude pact'. This legal phrase describes a contract made
without a consideration – that is, without passing something of
value sufficient to make the contract binding and therefore
resulting in no contract at all. In Roman law, *nudus* was used to
describe either a promise made without formal agreement or a type
of ownership that did not include the right to convey a property to
others.


**nulla dies sine linea**
you've got to keep at it

This expression, applied by Pliny to the Greek painter Apelles (see
*ne supra crepidam sutor iudicaret*), described the painter's
admirable steadfastness in practising his art. It is translated
literally as 'not a day without a line'.


**nulli secundus**
second to none


**nullius filius**
a bastard

Literally 'no one's son'.

**nullum quod tetigit non ornavit**
he touched nothing he did not adorn

From Dr Johnson's epitaph on Goldsmith: 'To Oliver Goldsmith, A Poet, Naturalist, and Historian, who left scarcely any style of writing untouched, and touched none [a better translation of *nullum*] he did not adorn.'


**numerus clausus**
a quota

This ugly phrase, literally 'closed number', veils in Latin the idea of limiting membership of classes of people deemed undesirable for a club, school or the like. 'When a *numerus clausus* is condoned for any group, your group may be next.'


**nunc aut nunquam**
now or never

An excellent phrase for anyone to use when trying to force someone into making a decision.


**nunc dimittis**
permission to leave

From Luke's Gospel: **nunc dimittis servum tuum, Domine**, 'Lord, now let thy servant depart'. To receive one's *nunc dimittis* is, therefore, to receive permission to depart.


**nunc est bibendum**
break out the champagne

Horace's call to merrymaking, literally 'Now it's time to drink', from the *Odes*.


**nunc pro tunc**
now for then

A wage settlement or other agreement made *nunc pro tunc* is retroactive to some time prior to the date of the settlement.

**nunc scripsi totum pro Christo da mihi potum**
Now I have written so much for Christ, give me a drink!

With this inscription, monk-copyists marked the end of a manuscript or perhaps the end of a day's work.


**nunquam non paratus**
never unprepared

A less direct way to say *semper paratus*.

### obiit
he or she died

An inscription found on tombstones and in church records. All that remains to be done is to supply the date of the unhappy event.

### obiit sine prole
he or she died without issue

Even unhappier than the preceding entry.

### obiter dictum
an incidental remark

A legal phrase, designating a statement made in passing by a judge on a tangential matter in connection with a judicial opinion he is rendering. While an *obiter dictum* – the plural is *obiter dicta* – has no legal bearing on the opinion to which it is appended, it may have considerable effect in later cases, since it may be read and considered along with the full opinion, and in some circumstances become even more important that the opinion itself.

### obsta principiis
nip it in the bud

Ovid advises in *Remedia Amoris* that we take immediate steps, literally that we 'resist the beginnings', once we know we have fallen into difficulties. It is much easier to root out evil as soon as it appears than to try to do so after its effects have become pervasive.

**obstupui, steteruntque comae, et vox faucibus haesit**
I was scared stiff

A description of the physical effects of fear, from Virgil's *Aeneid*, literally 'I was stupefied, and my hair stood on end, and my voice stuck to my throat.' How about that?


**occasionem cognosce**
strike while the iron is hot

Literally 'Recognize opportunity'.


**oderint dum metuant**
let them hate, provided they fear

A motto attributed to Emperor Tiberius, now appropriate for any despot or misguided business executive.


**odi et amo**
I hate and I love

Catullus, verbalizing the love-hate relationship. His thoughts continue: 'I don't know why, and I am in agony.'


**odi profanum vulgus et arceo**
I hate the common herd and stand aloof

Horace, in the *Odes*.


**odium**
hatred

This word plays a part in several Latin phrases of interest. **Odium aestheticum** designates the bitter rivalry among artists and writers; **odium medicum**, the hatred of physicians for one another – consider the attitude of the medical establishment toward radical practitioners; **odium theologicum**, mutual hatred among theologians, the result of differences in doctrinal interpretation.

**O fortunatos nimium, sua si bona norint, agricolas.**
Oh, blessed beyond all bliss, the farmers – did they but know their happiness.

Virgil, in the *Georgics*, apparently expressing a romantic view of bucolic life. In fairness to Virgil, the farmers he had in mind in this characterization were not perceived as blessed because of the nature of their work or their surroundings but because they were far removed from the dangers experienced by warriors.


**oleo tranquillior**
smoother than oil

An interesting phrase from the Psalms: 'His mouth was as smooth as butter, but his heart was war; his words were smoother than oil, yet they were drawn swords.'


**olet lucernam**
it smells of the lamp

Any laboured literary work may be condemned with this phrase, also given as **redolet lucernam**. So while students are advised to burn the midnight oil, poets and other creative writers must avoid giving the impression that they have laboured too long over a piece of work. (See *oleum perdisti*.)


**oleum addere camino**
to make bad things worse

Literally 'to pour fuel on the stove'.


**oleum perdisti**
you've wasted your time

Like *olet lucernam*, this phrase refers to the oil lamps used by Romans, this time in the literal meaning 'You have lost oil', telling a writer that whatever oil he burned while working on a manuscript was ill spent. A useful phrase for anyone intent on critical attack.

**olim meminisse iuvabit** (or **juvabit**)
It will be pleasant to look back on things past

Shades of Shakespeare and Proust:
  When to the sessions of sweet silent thought
  I summon up remembrance of things past ...
(See *forsan et haec olim meminisse iuvabit*.)


**omne ignotum pro magnifico est**
distance lends enchantment

Tacitus, in *Agricola*, gives us this useful phrase, literally 'Everything unknown is thought magnificent'. But it can also be interpreted as 'Everything unknown is thought to be more difficult or challenging than it really is'.


**omnem movere lapidem**
keep trying

This saying, literally 'to move every stone' or 'to leave no stone unturned', adjures us to do our level best in any enterprise.


**omnes deteriores sumus licentia**
too much freedom debases us

A saying attributed to Terence. Applied to child-rearing, these words recall 'Spare the rod and spoil the child'.


**omne trinum est perfectum**
everything in threes is perfect

An old adage, reflecting the mystical power ascribed to the number three. Three fates, three graces, three muses, the Trinity, three kings, Jonah in the whale's belly for three days and three nights, three cardinal colours, three cheers – the list is a long one.


**omne tulit punctum qui miscuit utile dulci**
he has gained every point who has combined the useful with the agreeable

Horace, in *Ars Poetica*.

**omnia mutantur nos et mutamur in illis**
all things change, and we change with them

Unless we want to be left behind.

**omnia vincit amor**
love conquers all

See *amor vincit omnia*.

**omnia vincit labor**
work conquers all things

See *labor omnia vincit*.

**onus probandi**
the burden of proof

Literally 'the burden of proving'.

**op. cit.**
See *opere citato*.

**ope et consilio**
with help and counsel

**opere citato**
in the work cited

Known better in its abbreviated form, **op. cit.**, this scholarly phrase is used in a footnote to indicate reference to a work previously cited. For example, 'Flexner, *op. cit.*, p. 242.'

**opere in medio**
in the midst of work

A useful phrase: 'You caught me *opere in medio.*'

**optat supremo collocare Sisyphus in monte saxum**
someone up there doesn't love me

The literal translation of this phrase is 'Sisyphus tries to place the boulder atop the mountain' but the phrase does not end there: **sed**

**vetant leges Iovis**, 'but Jove's decrees forbid'. Poor Sisyphus, mythological ruler of Corinth, was known for his cunning. In one version of the myth, the gods decided to punish him for showing disrespect to Zeus. They compelled him forever to push a boulder to the top of a mountain. Each time Sisyphus tried, he moved it closer to the top, but at the last moment the boulder would slip from his grasp and roll farther down the mountain from where he had started. Thus, when anyone is confronted with a task that seems to become harder and harder to complete, the task is termed Sisyphean. Have the gods taken offence?

**opus magnum**
a masterpiece

Literally 'a great work'. Also given as *magnum opus*.

**ora et labora**
pray and work

**ora pro nobis**
pray for us

**orator fit, poeta nascitur**
poets are born, not made

Literally 'An orator is made, a poet is born'.

**origo mali**
the source or origin of evil

Choose your own uses for this phrase.

**O si sic omnia**
oh, if everything were thus

A happy phrase for those rare times when one completes a task without a hitch, enjoys an ideal holiday or …

**O tempora! O mores!**
these are bad times

Literally, 'Oh, the times! Oh, the habits!' Speaking in the Roman
Senate, Cicero opened an attack on Catiline – he was accusing
Catiline of conspiracy – with a rhetorical question, 'How long will
you abuse our patience, Catiline?' and then exclaimed, '*O tempora!
O mores!*' The phrase has become a legacy for all who wish to
decry the times they live in.


**otium cum dignitate**
leisure with dignity

The best kind.

**pace tua**
with your permission

**Paete, non dolet**
don't worry, it doesn't hurt

Literally 'Paetus, it does not hurt'. The classic way to strengthen the wavering resolve of the second principal in a suicide pact to fulfil the rest of the agreement after the first member has taken the irretrievable step. Paetus, who had made the mistake of criticizing Emperor Nero, was number two in a husband-and-wife suicide pact. He watched while Arria, his wife, opened a vein in her arm. She then handed him the dagger and said, '*Paete, non dolet*.' It is an obvious advantage to know the right words to say under such circumstances.

**pallida Mors**
pale Death

The opening words of a sobering observation from Horace's *Odes*: 'Pale Death with impartial foot knocks at the doors of poor men's lodgings and of king's castles.'

**panem et circenses**
bread and circuses

Juvenal said that the Romans, once rulers of the world, had come to care for nothing but hand-outs and spectacles, and *panem et circenses* was the favourite formula for Roman leaders who wanted to keep the allegiance of the masses.

**pares cum paribus**
birds of a feather

The full expression is **pares cum paribus facillime congregantur**, with the literal meaning 'Like persons most readily crowd together'.

**pari passu**
at an equal pace

Two or more projects being worked on simultaneously and receiving an equal degree of attention – or inattention – may be said to be worked on *pari passu*.

**pari ratione**
by equally valid reasoning

Literally 'for a like reason'. 'Having explained at length why neither political candidate was acceptable to her, she concluded her statement with, "*Pari ratione*, I won't go to vote." '

**par pari refero**
tit for tat

Literally 'I return like for like'. (See *lex talionis*.)

**particeps criminis**
an accomplice

Literally 'a partner in the crime'.

**parturient montes, nascetur ridiculus mus**
all that work and nothing to show for it

Literally 'Mountains will be in labour, and an absurd mouse will be born', Horace's pungent line from *Ars Poetica*. An apt way to derogate a long-awaited novel, an expensive West End production, a much-discussed new building, a monumental piece of sculpture or the like that fails to live up to expectations.

**parva leves capiunt animas**
small minds concern themselves with trifles

Literally 'Small things occupy light minds', one of Ovid's lines in *Ars Amatoria*, and an apt comment when one is offended by pettiness.

**passim**
here and there

A scholarly reference, also translated as 'in various places' or 'in many places'. *Passim* informs the reader that the topic under discussion is treated in various places in a book or article that has been cited. For example, 'Chapter 4 *passim*' indicates that the topic is discussed here and there in the entire chapter; 'Chapter 4 *et passim*' indicates that the topic is discussed in Chapter 4 as well as here and there throughout the rest of the work.

**paterfamilias**
a patriarch

Literally 'father of a family'. *Paterfamilias* can also be taken as 'head of a household'. (See *materfamilias*.)

**Pater Noster**
Our Father

The opening words of the Lord's Prayer, in Latin called the *Paternoster*: 'Our Father, which art in heaven ...'

**pater patriae**
father of his country

The Romans sometimes used this expression to designate distinguished statesmen.

**patris est filius**
a chip off the old block

Literally 'He is his father's son'.

**pauca sed bona**
few things, but good

An excellent precept for Christmas shoppers.


**paucis verbis**
in brief

Literally 'in few words'.


**paupertas omnium artium repertrix**
necessity is the mother of invention

Literally 'Poverty is the inventor of all the arts'.


**pax**
peace

This Latin word gives us the core of many expressions. **Pax Britannica**, literally 'the peace of Britain', reflects the terms imposed by the British on members of their colonial empire. **Pax in bello** is 'peace in war', a peace in which fighting continues but at a reduced rate. **Pax regis** is 'the king's peace'. **Pax Romana**, literally 'the Roman peace', denotes the peace dictated by the impressive strength of the Roman military. **Pax vobiscum** is a greeting, literally 'Peace be unto you'. Christ greeted the apostles with these words on the first Easter morning. **Pax tecum** is the singular form of *pax vobiscum*.


**peccavi**
I have sinned

The pleasurable aspect of this frank admission, normally made in the confessional (see *mea culpa*), lies in its use in a dispatch by Sir Charles Napier, a British general, while on campaign in 1843 in north-west India. Having taken Miani, in central Sind, he wrote the single word *Peccavi* as his entire message to his superiors, announcing conquest – in actuality at that point still incomplete – of the entire region. Listen closely: *Peccavi*. (I have sinned? No, I have Sind.)

**pecunia non olet**
money doesn't smell

A Roman proverb counselling us not to concern ourselves with the source of any money that may come our way. Don't look a gift horse in the mouth.

**pecunia obediunt omnia**
money makes the world go round

Literally 'All things yield to money'. *Obediunt* is also seen as *oboediunt*.

**penates**
household gods

See *lares et penates*.

**pendente lite**
while the suit is pending

A legal phrase. '*Pendente lite*, I shall say make no public statements.'

**penetralia mentis**
heart of hearts

Literally 'the innermost recesses of the mind'.

**per acria belli**
through the harshness of war

The word *acria* may also be translated as 'bitterness' or 'savagery'.

**per angusta ad augusta**
through difficulties to honours

Also given as *ad augusta per angusta*.

**per annum**
annually

Literally 'by the year'.

**per ardua ad astra**
through difficulties to the stars

Motto of the Royal Air Force. The thought is also conveyed by *per aspera ad astra*. (See *ad astra per aspera*.)

**per capita**
individually

Literally 'by the head'.

**per centum**
on each hundred

Literally 'by the hundred'.

**per contra**
on the contrary

This expression is used today most often to mean 'on the opposite side of the argument'.

**per diem**
daily

Literally 'by the day'.

**per fas et nefas**
justly or unjustly

Literally 'through right and wrong'. 'This is what I plan to do, *per fas et nefas.*'

**periculum in mora**
danger in delay

A good expression to use when counselling against inaction.

**per impossibile**
as is impossible

An elegant way to qualify a proposition that cannot now or ever be true: 'Assume, *per impossibile*, that you were born in Shakespeare's time.'

**per incuriam**
through want of care.

Characterizing a mistaken decision of a court.

**per interim**
meanwhile

The English noun *interim* is visible here.

**per Iovem** (or **Jovem**)
by Jupiter

Also rendered in English by the phrase 'by Jove', Jove being another name for Jupiter.

**per mensem**
monthly

**per minas**
by threats

**permitte divis cetera**
leave the rest to the gods

Horace gives us this line in the *Odes*, suggesting that there is just so much we can do to order our lives, make our plans and the like. 'When you have done all you can in the interest of prudence, *permitte divis cetera* and take the plunge.'

**per se**
intrinsically

Literally 'by or in itself'.


**persona grata**
an acceptable person

While this term can be taken to mean 'a welcome guest' or 'a favourite person', it is most generally used to describe a diplomatic representative who is acceptable to the government to which he or she is accredited. When a diplomat is no longer *persona grata*, he or she becomes **persona non grata**.


**persta atque obdura**
be steadfast and endure


**pessimum genus inimicorum laudantes**
flatterers are the worst type of enemies


**petitio principii**
begging the question

The logical fallacy, literally 'begging of the principle', of taking for granted that which remains to be proved. For example, stating as a matter of proof that parallel lines will never meet because they are parallel assumes as fact the very thought one is supposed to prove.


**pictor ignotus**
painter unknown

A way of indicating an anonymous work of art.


**pinxit**
he (or she) painted it

This word, preceded by the name of the artist, is found on many old paintings.

**placet**
it pleases

Used as an affirmative vote or an expression of assent. (See *non placet*.)

**plaudite, cives**
let's give them a hand!

Literally 'Applaud, citizens', *plaudite, cives* was the call addressed to an audience at the end of a Roman play.

**plures crapula quam gladius**
more people die at parties than fighting wars

The Romans knew the toll taken by over-indulgence. This grim expression translates literally as 'Drunkenness (kills) more than the sword'.

**poeta nascitur, non fit**
a poet is born, not made

See *orator fit, poeta nascitur* for yet another reminder for unpublished poets

**pollice verso**
thumbs down

When a gladiator in a Roman amphitheatre had an opponent at his mercy, he customarily looked toward the spectators for guidance on whether to administer the *coup de grâce*. If the spectators turned their thumbs toward their chest – *pollice verso*, literally 'with thumb turned' – they were making clear that they wanted to see the opponent killed. If they wanted the opponent to live, they kept their thumbs in their fists – **pollice compresso**, literally 'with thumb folded'. Our modern phrases of approval and disapproval, 'thumbs up' and 'thumbs down', do not ordinarily apply to situations of life and death, but they may derive from the Roman practice.

**posse comitatus**
a posse

Western fans will be pleased to know that a *posse comitatus*, literally 'the power of a county', is the full phrase from which derives the word 'posse'. Members of any self-respecting posse – in reality, too often a group of vigilantes – are enlisted on the spot by a sheriff just after the local bank has been robbed or some other outrage has been committed. Fortunately, everyone in a Hollywood Western has a horse to ride on and a rifle to fire at the bad guys, who are heading for the hills and soon will be ensconced behind boulders that will prove no more than a temporary barrier against the bullets of the posse's guns.

**possunt quia posse videntur**
they can do it because they think they can do it

The power of positive thinking, as expressed by Virgil in the *Aeneid*, with the literal meaning 'They can because they seem to be able to'. The appearance of power bestows power.

**post equitem sedet atra cura**
behind the horseman sits black care

One of the less appealing thoughts from Horace's *Odes*. The implication is that no one is free of anxiety.

**post festum venisti**
sorry, too late!

Literally 'You have arrived after the feast'. This expression can be invoked whenever the overly cautious have let opportunity slip through their fingers. (See *carpe diem*.)

**post hoc, ergo propter hoc**
after this, therefore because of this

The logical fallacy that because one event follows another, the former must have caused the latter. For example, ingestion of a large quantity of vitamin C upon the first sign of a cold may well be followed by complete remission of cold symptoms, yet the true explanation of the phenomenon could lie elsewhere: a mistaken diagnosis, removal of an offending allergen, an improvement in astrological signs – heaven knows what. But until the jury returns on this one, perhaps it's better to take the megadose and risk the consequences of *post hoc, ergo propter hoc*.

## post meridiem
after noon

The phrase we all know in its abbreviated form, PM. (See *ante meridiem*.)

## post mortem
an autopsy

Literally 'after death'.

## post nubila Phoebus
every cloud has a silver lining

Literally 'After clouds, Phoebus'. Phoebus, one of the names for Apollo, god of the sun, was used by poets to mean 'the sun'.

## post partum
after childbirth

The period after delivery of a child. In English, we may hear of 'postpartum depression'. (See *ante partum*.)

## post scriptum
written afterward

Better known as PS.

## potius mori quam foedari
death before dishonour

Literally 'rather to die than to be dishonoured'. Whenever one expresses oneself in this vein, there is a tendency to run wild.

**praemonitus praemunitus**
forewarned, forearmed

**praestat sero quam nunquam**
better late than never

**prima facie**
at first sight

This phrase, which finds frequent use in the law, can be taken as 'at first view or appearance' or 'on first consideration'. It suggests that thorough investigation has not been conducted, but an inference can be drawn that appears to be valid: 'Notes found in the possession of a student sitting for an examination are considered *prima facie* evidence of intent to cheat.' In law, therefore, a *prima facie* case is one based on facts legally sufficient to establish the case unless the facts presented are disproved.

**primus inter pares**
the first among equals

This paradoxical phrase finds use in describing the pecking order within a group of males of equal rank. The full professors in a university department are a good example. No individual professor stands above the others in rank, but the professor who is designated chairman may be said while holding that position to be *primus inter pares*. While he may not dismiss or otherwise affect the careers of the other professors, since they all are of equal rank, for the period of his chairmanship he presides over departmental meetings and has certain prerogatives not enjoyed by the others. There is a corresponding Latin phrase for a woman who is first among equals: **prima inter pares**.

**probitas laudatur et alget**
honesty is praised and is neglected

A cynical observation from Juvenal's *Satires*, sometimes rendered as 'Virtue is praised and then left to freeze'. The implication is clear: society may approve goodness of character but won't reward it.

**pro bono publico**
for the public good

The full phrase for the expression **pro bono** often heard these days.

**profanum vulgus**
the common people

Literally 'the profane multitude'. (See *mobile vulgus*.)

**pro forma**
as a formality

Literally 'for form'. 'They made a *pro forma* appeal for a stay of execution, knowing they had little chance of saving their client's life.'

**promotor fidei**
promoter of the faith

See *advocatus diaboli*.

**pro patria**
for one's country

Literally 'for the country'.

**proprio motu**
by one's own initiative

Literally 'on one's own motion'.

**proprium humani ingenii est odisse quem laeseris**
it is human nature to hate a person whom you have injured

An insightful observation from Tacitus, in the *Agricola*.

**pro rata**
in proportion

**prosit**
cheers!

A Latin toast, literally 'May it benefit you' but freely translatable as 'To you', 'Your good fortune', 'To life' – and any of the multitude of expressions we use to wish someone good health when we lift a glass of spirits or, in these times, a glass of white wine. Perrier water does not qualify.

**pro tempore**
temporarily

The full phrase for **pro tem**. A chairperson *pro tem* is chairperson *pro tempore*, to serve until a permanent chairperson is selected.

**proxime accessit**
he or she came nearest

See *accessit*.

**PS**
See *post scriptum*.

**punctatim**
point for point

**Punica fides**
treachery

This ironic phrase, which translates literally as 'Punic [Carthaginian] faith', reflects the Roman attitude toward their rivals in the Punic Wars. (See *delenda est Carthago*.)

**QED**
Abbreviation of *quod erat demonstrandum*.


**QEF**
Abbreviation of *quod erat faciendum*.


**qua**
in the capacity of

A form of the pronoun **qui**, literal meaning 'who'. 'He puts his duties *qua* citizen above other loyalties.'


**quae nocent docent**
things that hurt teach

The rhyming way to indicate the educational validity of the curriculum offered by the College of Hard Knocks.


**quaerenda pecunia primum est, virtus post nummos**
let's keep our eye on the bottom line

A practical thought from Horace's *Epistles*, with the literal meaning 'Money is the first thing to be sought, good reputation after wealth'.


**quaere verum**
seek the truth

**qualis artifex pereo**
what an artist dies in me

Suetonius reports that Nero – he who is said to have fiddled while Rome burned – spoke these words shortly before committing suicide. While Nero is known to have loved music, there is no indication that he was a man of great talent.

**qualis pater talis filius**
like father, like son

**quando hic sum, non ieiuno (or jejuno) Sabbato;**
**quando Romae sum, ieiuno (or jejuno) Sabbato**
when in Rome, do as the Romans do

The Latin for this thought is rendered in various ways, but the thought is always attributed to St Ambrose. The version supplied above may be translated literally as 'When I'm here [in Milan], I do not fast on Saturday; when I'm in Rome, I fast on Saturday.' No matter how the Latin reads, the advice is the same: follow local customs.

**quandoque bonus dormitat Homerus**
sometimes even good Homer sleeps

(See *aliquando bonus dormitat Homerus*.)

**quantum**
as much

This word gives us several useful phrases. **Quantum libet**, 'as much as one pleases'. **Quantum meruit**, 'as much as one has deserved'. **Quantum placeat**, 'as much as pleases'. **Quantum satis**, 'as much as is sufficient'. **Quantum sufficit**, 'as much as suffices'. **Quantum valeat**, 'as much as it may be worth'. **Quantum vis**, 'as much as you wish'.

**quare impedit?**
why is he fighting us?

Literally 'Why does he obstruct?'

**quem di diligunt, adolescens moritur**
only the good die young

The literal translation of this consoling line is 'Whom the gods love dies young'. *Quem di diligunt, adolescens moritur* is a translation into Latin made by Plautus in the *Bacchides* of a line by Menander, a fourth-century BC Greek dramatist.

**qui bene amat bene castigat**
he who loves well chastises well

The Latin argument opposing permissiveness in raising children and favouring frankness of expression in dealing with all people one loves or respects.

**qui desiderat pacem praeparet bellum**
let him who wants peace prepare for war

Vegetius, a Roman military writer, advocating anything but arms control.

**quid faciendum?**
what's to be done?

**quid novi?**
what's new?

**quid nunc?**
what now?

This phrase gives us the English word 'quidnunc', 'a busybody'.

**qui docet discit**
the best way to learn a subject is to teach it

Literal translation, 'He who teaches learns'. Every experienced teacher knows the truth of this aphorism.

**quid pro quo**
something given in return for something

Literally 'something for something'. 'I will not give up that privilege without a *quid pro quo*.'


**quidquid agas prudenter agas**
whatever you do, do with caution

See *respice finem*.


**qui fugiebat rursus proeliabitur**
he who fights and runs away may live to fight another day

Tertullian, quoting a Greek source on the futility of making a last-ditch stand when the odds are heavily against one. The Latin may be translated literally as 'He who has fled will do battle once more'. The rendering given above is Oliver Goldsmith's.


**qui me amat, amat et canem meam**
love me, love my dog

The Latin words for telling the world that it will have to take you as you are. The literal translation is 'Who loves me loves my dog as well'.


**qui nescit dissimulare nescit vivere**
he who doesn't know how to fib doesn't know how to survive

More formally, 'He who does not know how to dissemble does not know how to live'. This same Latin line, with the last word replaced by **regnare** ('to rule'), may give us some insight into the way nations large and small are governed.


**qui scribit bis legit**
he who writes reads twice

This maxim recognizes the effectiveness of writing out something one wishes to learn thoroughly.

## quis custodiet ipsos custodes?
who will guard the guards themselves?

Juvenal, in his *Satires*, poses this vexing question, suitable today for situations in which we have little confidence in the people appointed to positions of trust – for example, those who are duty-bound to watch over public funds. Juvenal may actually have been more concerned with the problem of hiring guards to prevent infidelity among women whose husbands were out of town. The modern challenge more likely is to avoid assignment of a fox to guard the henhouse.

## quis fallere possit amantem?
who can deceive a lover?

Virgil, in the *Aeneid*, giving us wisdom about the human condition.

## qui tacet consentit
silence implies consent

Literally 'He who remains silent consents'. This observation may be applied to a range of situations, from silence at an everyday business meeting to silence of an entire people in a country that is pursuing an inhumane policy.

## qui timide rogat docet negare
don't be afraid to ask

Literally 'He who asks timidly teaches to refuse'. In better translation, 'He who asks timidly invites refusal'.

## quo animo?
with what intention?

Even when we report all the words someone has used in telling us something, we may not be conveying a true reflection of what was intended. Facial expression, emphasis and the like may be as significant as the words themselves in revealing the full story. Thus, we are not surprised when we are asked, '*Quo animo?*'

**quod avertat Deus!**
God forbid!

Literally 'which may God avert'.


**quod cibus est aliis, aliis est venenum**
one man's meat is another man's poison

Literally 'What is food to some is poison to others'. What you and I find attractive, others may well find abhorrent. (See *de gustibus non est disputandum.*)


**quod cito acquiritur cito perit**
easy come, easy go

Literally 'That which is quickly acquired quickly vanishes'.


**quod erat demonstrandum**
which was to be demonstrated

The statement, abbreviated QED, that is appended to a mathematical solution, with the meaning 'We have proved the proposition we set out to prove'.


**quod erat faciendum**
which was to be done

The statement, abbreviated QEF, that is appended to a mathematical solution, with the meaning 'We have done the work we were required to do'.


**quod vide**
which see

See *q.v.*


**quo iure (or jure)?**
by what right?

A challenge: 'Why have you done this?' *or* 'What have you done?' '*Quo iure?*'

**quomodo vales?**
how are you?

A Roman greeting.

**quondam**
former

Used in English: 'my quondam [erstwhile] friend'.

**quorum**
of whom

Given here primarily to show the origin of the English noun *quorum*, 'the minimum number of people that must be present at a meeting before its proceedings are to be regarded as valid'. In commissions written in Latin appeared the words **quorum vos ... unum [duos** etc.] **esse volumus**, 'of whom we will that you ... be one [two etc.].' The intent was to designate the person (or persons) so addressed as member (or members) of an official body, without whose presence work could not go on. And that's how *quorum* was born.

**quos Deus vult perdere prius dementat**
whom God wishes to destroy, he first makes mad

A Latin rendering of a line from Euripides.

**quot homines, tot sententiae**
complete lack of agreement

A phrase from Terence's *Phormio*, literally 'so many men, so many opinions', leaving one as far from consensus as possible.

**quo vadis?**
whither goest thou?

The well-known question from John's Gospel.

**q.v.**

The abbreviation of **quod vide**, literally 'which see', a scholar's way of providing a cross-reference. For example, '*quondam, q.v.*'

indicates to the reader who does not know the meaning of *quondam* that the term is explained elsewhere in the text, in the case of the present book in its alphabetical location.

**radit usque ad cutem**
he drives a hard bargain

Literally 'He shaves all the way to the skin'.


**radix omnium malorum est cupiditas**
the love of money is the root of all evil

Please notice that this observation from the New Testament Book of Timothy is concerned not with wealth but with avarice: money *per se* is not the root of evil.


**rara avis**
a rarity

A prodigy or anything that is quite out of the ordinary may be described as a *rara avis*, literally 'a rare bird'. Juvenal used the phrase in his *Satires*: **rara avis in terris nigroque simillima cycno**, 'a rare bird upon the earth and very much like a black swan'. Black swans were unknown to the Romans. They were discovered in modern times.


**raram facit misturam cum sapientia forma**
beauty and brains don't mix

We have Petronius's *Satyricon* to blame for this canard, literally 'Beauty and wisdom are rarely found together'. The myth of 'beautiful but dumb' is destroyed by university teachers each time they look up from their notes. What they see is a lecture hall filled with intelligent and attractive students. What the students see may be another matter.

**re**
concerning or regarding

**rebus sic stantibus**
as matters stand

A phrase, literally 'things staying as they are', that lawyers use as one criterion for determining that an obligation or a contract remains in force.

**recte et suaviter**
justly and mildly

**recto**
right

This term is used to denote a right-hand page of a book, the full Latin phrase being **recto folio**, 'the page being straight'. See *verso*.

**reddite quae sunt Caesaris Caesari, et quae sunt Dei Deo**
render unto Caesar the things that are Caesar's, and unto God the things that are God's

Matthew recounting Christ's response to the Pharisees, who asked whether they should pay tribute to the Romans.

**redime te captum quam queas minimo**
only name, rank, and serial number

The Latin prescription for soldierly behaviour following capture by enemy troops, literally 'When taken prisoner, pay as little as you can to buy your freedom'. In ancient times, the enemy wanted money, not information, but the principle was the same: give the enemy as little help as possible.

**redivivus**
brought back to life

This word gives us an opportunity to call 'a second Beethoven' a Beethoven *redivivus* – and probably be wrong in both languages.

**redolet lucernam**
it's laboured

This destructive phrase may be used by critics to convey the literal thought 'It smells of the lamp', suggesting that a composer or writer stayed up nights – that is, worked too hard – to create the work. The implication is that genius doesn't sweat in creating a masterpiece – do you believe it? When critics have exhausted the possibilities of this phrase, they can always describe a work of art as 'careless'. (See *olet lucernam*.)

**reductio ad absurdum**
reduction to absurdity

Disproof of a principle or proposition by showing that it leads to an absurdity when followed to its logical conclusion.

**regina**
queen

**rem acu tetigisti**
right on!

Where the old-fashioned among us might say, 'You've hit the nail right on the head', Romans would have said *rem acu tetigisti*, literally 'You've touched the thing with a needle'.

**remis velisque**
giving one's best

Literally 'with oars and sails', a phrase that reminds us that the aeroplane is a modern invention. 'He took out after them *remis velisque*.'

**repente dives nemo factus est bonus**
no one who is rich is made suddenly good

Publilius Syrus, as shown in this aphorism, was a keen observer of people and their ways. The intent of his observation applies even now: when someone you know appears to have made a sudden improvement in his style of living, don't be surprised if the law shows up one day to ask him embarrassing questions.

**requiescat in pace**
may he or she rest in peace

The plural form of this final thought is **requiescant in pace**, 'May they rest in peace'. The abbreviation for both the singular and the plural is RIP.

**res age, tute eris**
wash that man right out of your hair

Ovid gives advice to the lovelorn in *Remedia Amoris*, saying literally 'Be busy and you will be safe'.

**res angusta domi**
Daddy has lost his job

This sad statement, literally 'straitened circumstances at home', is useful in itself, but one may also find it instructive to recall a line from Juvenal's *Satires* in which the words appear: **Haud facile emergunt quorum virtutibus opstat res angusta domi**, 'By no means is it easy for those to rise from obscurity whose noble qualities are hindered by straitened circumstances at home.' Juvenal, in expressing concern for the unfortunate among us, was far ahead of many hard-nosed people in positions of power today, who insist that the poor have only themselves to blame.

**res in cardine est**
the next twenty-four hours will tell the story

Literally 'The matter is on a door hinge' or, as we are apt to say more conventionally, 'We are facing a crisis.'

**res inter alios**
it's no concern of ours

Literally 'a matter between other people'.

**res ipsa loquitur**
The facts speak for themselves

Literally 'The thing itself speaks'. A complainant in a car accident case who appears in court swathed in bandages and escorted by nurses should not have to go to great lengths to establish that he has been injured: *res ipsa loquitur*.

## respice finem
look before you leap

Literally 'Examine the end'. The full proverb, **quidquid agas prudenter agas et respice finem**, may be translated as 'Whatever you do, do with caution, and look to the end.'

## respondeat superior
the buck stops here

The tradition of accountability, literally 'Let the superior answer', more freely 'A supervisor must take responsibility for the quality of a subordinate's work'.

## res publica
the commonwealth

Literally 'the affairs of the people'. What the Romans meant when they said *res publica* – it is the origin of the English word 'republic' – was 'the state' (in the sense of 'the body politic'), 'the republic' or, as given above, 'the commonwealth'. However interpreted, by *res publica*, the Romans meant their own commonwealth. *Res publica* was also written as a single word, **respublica**.

## resurgam
I shall rise again

## retro Satana!
get thee behind me, Satan!

The abbreviated form of *vade retro me, Satana*. (See also *apage Satanas*.)

**rex non potest peccare**
the king can do no wrong

**rex regum**
king of kings

**RIP**
See *requiescat in pace.*

**ruat caelum**
come what may

Literally 'though the heavens fall'. (See *fiat iustitia ruat caelum.*)

**rus in urbe**
country in city

The phrase is used most often to describe a city building, garden or view that suggests the countryside. 'They gave up their *rus in urbe* overlooking Hyde Park for a flat on Oxford Street.' *Rus in urbe* is also used, but less often, to denote the creating of an illusion of countryside in a city setting. 'In her designs for urban buildings, she specializes in *rus in urbe.*'

**sal Atticum**
wit

This phrase from Pliny's *Historia Naturalis*, often given in English as 'Attic wit', is literally 'Attic salt', reflecting the refined elegance, the taste – no pun is intended – of the ancient Athenian (Attic) intelligentsia. The wit denoted is often taken as 'acerbity' or 'intellectual wit'. Byron, in his *English Bards and Scotch Reviewers*, referred to a taste for punning as 'Attic salt'.

**salus mundi**
the welfare of the world

**salus populi suprema lex esto**
let the welfare of the people be the supreme law

Cicero, in *De Legibus*, had it this way: **Salus populi suprema est lex**, 'The welfare of the people is the supreme law.'

**salus ubi multi consiliarii**
where there are many advisers there is safety

An excellent reminder for politicians whose words and actions hold hostage the future of the world. (See *salus mundi*.)

**salve!**
hail!

A Roman greeting.

**sanctum sanctorum**
a place of inviolable privacy

*Sanctum* in English is a noun meaning 'a retreat or a private room'. In Latin, *sanctum* is a neuter adjective meaning 'sacred'. Combining the Latin *sanctum* with *sanctorum* gives us a phrase that can be translated literally as 'holy of holies', useful in denoting a place in a house of worship proscribed for all but the high priests, or a room in a home that is off limits to everyone but the master or mistress – either one, not both – of the establishment.


**sapiens nihil affirmat quod non probat**
don't swear to anything you don't know firsthand

Excellent advice, translated literally as 'A wise man states as true nothing he does not prove'.


**Sartor Resartus**
*The Tailor Reclothed*

Title of a book by Thomas Carlyle that examines life under the guise of expounding a philosophy of clothing. Not to be confused with *Dress for Success* or others of that ilk.


**satis**
enough

*Satis* gives us several interesting phrases. **Satis superque**, 'enough and to spare'. *Satis verborum*, 'enough of words'; by extension: 'Let's have some action.' The most satisfying is **satis eloquentiae, sapientiae parum**, 'enough eloquence, too little wisdom'. Ah, the joys of Latin.


**Saturnalia**
an orgy

We know the English word 'saturnalia' as 'unrestrained revelry' but the Latin original is worth reviewing. The *Saturnalia* was the week-long Roman festival said to have begun in mid-December – sometimes given as the 17th of the month, sometimes as the 19th. The nature of the festival is not in dispute: public spectacles and banquets, freedom from restraint, general merrymaking, debauchery and exchanges of presents. Indeed, during *Saturnalia* masters waited on slaves, courts and schools were closed, and sentencing of criminals was suspended. Who could ask for anything more? And all this in honour of Saturn, in Latin *Saturnus*, the god of planting and harvest, among other things.

**scientia est potentia**
knowledge is power

An appropriate maxim for illicit wiretappers and those who record their telephone conversations without informing the people they speak with that they are doing so.

**scilicet**
namely

Used in English in place of 'to wit'. *Scilicet* is the Latin abbreviation of **scire licet**, 'it is permitted to know'.

**scripsit**
he (or she) wrote it

With the author's name given first, a way to sign a literary work.

**sculpsit**
he (or she) carved (or cut) it

With the artisan's name given first, a way to sign a carving, engraving etc.

**semel insanivimus omnes**
we have all been mad once

A good point to keep in mind when dealing with someone who has committed an anti-social act or made an egregious error. No one goes through life without slipping now and then.

**semper fidelis**
always faithful

**semper idem**
always the same thing

A descriptive phrase suitable for characterizing something or someone whose appearance does not change.

**semper paratus**
always ready

**Senatus Populusque Romanus**
the Roman Senate and People

Abbreviated SPQR and, for the Romans, emblematic of their constitution.

**senex bis puer**
second childhood

This disagreeable Latin phrase, evocative of Shakespeare's characterization of the final stage of man – he called it 'second childishness' – literally translates as 'An old man is twice a boy'.

**seniores priores**
elders first

A civilized precept.

**seq.**

Abbreviation of **sequens** and **sequentes**, respectively the singular and plural forms meaning 'the following', and of **sequitur** (see the next entry). The plural of *seq.* is sometimes written as *seqq*.

**sequitur**
it follows

This word can be used to mean 'It follows logically' (see *non sequitur*) or to mean 'the following remark'.

**seriatim**
in series

A scholar's term, used to indicate that a publication is part of a series.

**sero venientibus ossa**
sorry, too late

The Latin version of 'The early bird catches the worm'. Literally 'for latecomers, the bones'. (See *post festum venisti*.)

**sesquipedalia verba**
oppressively long words

The English word 'sesquipedalian' is an adjective carrying the meanings 'having many syllables' and 'tending to use long words'. The Latin phrase, from Horace's *Ars Poetica*, literally means 'words a foot and a half long'. If Horace was referring to metrical feet, the phrase would describe words having at least four or five syllables, but he could also have had linear measure in mind, in which event the length of such words would boggle the mind. In either case, the meaning is clear, and Horace has given us an excellent way to characterize writers whose vocabularies are so pretentious that their readers must go repeatedly to an unabridged dictionary in order to understand what they are reading. *Sesquipedalia verba* may also be used to characterize the writing of such authors.

**sic**
thus

This common word is used by writers and editors to indicate an apparent misspelling or a doubtful word or phrase in a source being quoted. 'This dessiccant [*sic*] is useless.' 'The meeting was the most fortuitous [*sic*] I ever attended.' Insertion of *sic* in these examples absolves the quoter of misspelling the word 'desiccant' and misusing the word 'fortuitous' and lays the blame – if blame it is – on the source quoted.

**sic itur ad astra**
this is the path to immortality

Literally 'Thus one goes to the stars'.

**sic semper tyrannis**
thus ever to tyrants

Motto of Virginia and said to be the words shouted by John Wilkes Booth after assassinating Abraham Lincoln. Booth is also said to have added, 'The South is avenged.'

**sic transit gloria mundi**
so passes away the glory of the world

Thomas à Kempis, in *De Imitatione Christi*, commenting on the transitory nature of human vanities. The Latin phrase is used at the coronation of a pope. A rope bundle is burned during the ceremony and, as the flame dies, the words '**Pater sancte** ("holy father") **sic transit gloria mundi**' are intoned.

**si des placet**
if it pleases the gods

The equivalent of 'God willing'. (See *deo volente*.)

**si fecisti nega!**
stonewall!

Literally 'If you did it, deny it'.

**si finis bonus est, totum bonum erit**
'all's well that ends well'

Literally 'If the end is good, everything will be good'. Shakespeare couldn't have said it better.

**sigillum**
a seal

**silent leges enim inter arma**
laws don't count in wartime

The principle used to justify imposition of martial law. This maxim, found in Cicero's *Pro Milone*, translates literally as 'For laws are silent in the midst of war'.

**similia similibus curantur**
fight fire with fire

Literally 'Like things are cured by likes', more freely 'Similar ailments are treated successfully by similar remedies'. This is the doctrine of homeopathy, which advocates treatment of a disease by giving the sick person small amounts of substances that would produce symptoms of the same disease if they were given to a healthy person. It is also the basis for the putative hair-of-the-dog cure of a hangover, in which the afflicted person is encouraged to imbibe small amounts of the same substance that caused the unfortunate condition in the first place. (See *contraria contrariis curantur*.)

**sine die**
until an unspecified date

When a meeting adjourns *sine die*, literally 'without a day', don't hold your breath until it reconvenes.

**sine dubio**
without doubt

**sine invidia**
without envy

**sine ira**
without anger

**sine loco et anno**
without place and date

A bibliographer's term. A book that does not provide information concerning its place and date of publication is said to have been published *sine loco et anno*. Modern books normally supply such information.

**sine mora**
without delay

**sine praeiudicio** (or **praejudicio**)
without prejudice

**sine prole**
without children

A legal term, often translated as 'without issue', encountered in some wills.

**sine qua non**
an indispensable condition, something that cannot be done without

Literally 'without which not'. Anything that may be described accurately as *sine qua non* is absolutely necessary. 'Warm outer clothing is a *sine qua non* at the North Pole.'

**si post fata venit gloria non propero**
if one must die to be recognized, I can wait

One of Martial's epigrams, literally 'If glory comes after death, I'm not in a hurry'. For a writer, this means 'better unread than dead'.

**si sic omnes**
why couldn't it last forever?

A wistful expression, literally 'If everything had been thus'.


**siste viator**
stop, traveller

A favourite inscription on Roman tombstones.


**sit non doctissima coniux** (or **conjux**)
a Roman formula for a happy marriage

One of Martial's epigrams, literally 'May my wife not be very learned', revealing more than we would like to know about one Roman's attitude toward women.


**sit tibi terra levis**
may the earth be light upon you

An ancient Roman tombstone inscription.


**si monumentum requiris, circumspice**
if you seek (his) monument, look around you

The inscription on the tomb of Sir Christopher Wren in St Paul's Cathedral, London, the finest work of this architect.


**si vis me flere dolendum est primum ipsi tibi**
if you wish me to weep, you yourself must first feel grief

Method acting? Horace, in *Ars Poetica*, explaining to the writer that emotion must be felt in order to be conveyed successfully in words.


**si vis pacem para bellum**
if you want peace, prepare for war

A traditional justification for an arms build-up, from Vegetius, a Roman military writer, in his *Epitoma Rei Militaris*.

**socius criminis**
a partner in crime

**soli Deo gloria**
glory to God alone

**sol lucet omnibus**
the sun shines for everyone

**spectatum veniunt, veniunt spectentur ut ipsae**
they wish as much to be seen as to see

An observation by Ovid, in *Ars Amatoria*, literally 'They come to see, they come that they themselves be seen', making it clear that the beautiful people have not changed much in two millennia.

**spolia optima**
how sweet it is!

This phrase, literally 'the choicest spoils', was used by Livy to denote the booty personally taken by a victorious general who has slain the commanding general of an enemy army.

**sponte sua**
of one's own accord

Usually given as **sua sponte**.

**SPQR**
Abbreviation of *Senatus Populusque Romanus*, 'the Roman Senate and People'. SPQR is often seen in depictions of Roman military standards.

**stans pede in uno**
effortlessly

Horace used this expression, literally 'standing on one foot', in his *Satires*. Some of us use the equivalent expression in English: 'I can do that standing on one foot.' Now we can do it *stans pede in uno*.

**status**
conditions or state

This Latin word, which can also be translated as 'status', is used commonly in a handful of Latin expressions: **statu quo**, 'as things were before'; **status quo**, 'the state in which anything is (or was)'; **status quo ante bellum**, 'the condition (or military boundaries) that existed before the war'; and **status quo ante**, an abbreviated version of the previous phrase, with the same meanings. 'Even though the couple had reunited, both husband and wife knew that too many recriminations had been exchanged, too much bitterness remained. They would never return to *status quo ante*.'

**stet**
let it stand

An editor or proof-reader's mark cancelling a deletion or other change previously made in a manuscript or proof. *Stet* also appears in various Latin expressions, including two of quite different intent. **Stet fortuna domus!** means 'May the good fortune of the house endure!' **Stet pro ratione voluntas** means 'Let my will stand as a reason', giving a person in command a way of dismissing any arguments advanced to question his judgement; in English, 'End of discussion. We'll do it my way.'

**stillicidi casus lapidem cavat**
slow and steady does it

A Roman proverb, literally 'Dripping moisture hollows out a stone'.

**stultorum calami carbones moenia chartae**
no graffiti, please

The Romans, in this saying, literally 'Chalk is the pen of fools, walls (their) paper', reveal that the graffiti artist is far from a modern phenomenon. Archaeologists have found graffiti on walls of buildings in many ancient Roman cities, including Pompeii, and the nature of the literary, artistic, political and cultural content revealed in these ancient graffiti does not vary substantially from what can be seen today in many cities. *O tempora! O mores!*

**sua cuique voluptas**
to each his own

Literally 'Everyone has his own pleasures'. A related expression is
**sua cuique sunt vitia**, Everyone has his own vices'.


**sua sponte**
of one's own accord

Sometimes given as **sponte sua**.


**suaviter in modo, fortiter in re**
he does what has to be done, but with the necessary compassion

In our everyday lives, we must inevitably do things we would
prefer not to do. It is then that we are called on to be *suaviter in
modo, fortiter in re*, literally 'gentle in manner, resolute in deed', or
to behave *suaviter in modo, fortiter in re*, literally 'gently in
manner, resolutely in deed'. Thus, *suaviter in modo, fortiter in re*
describes the model parent, executive, personnel manager *et al.*


**sub iudice** (or **judice**)
before the courts

When a matter is before the courts – that is, still under litigation –
the case generally is not discussed publicly by those directly
involved. The intent is to avoid prejudicing the legal process. (See
*adhuc sub iudice lis est.*)


**sub poena**
under penalty

Add 'of a fine' or 'of imprisonment' or what you will after this
phrase, and the result is threatening. The derivation of the English
noun 'subpoena', 'a writ commanding a person to appear in a law
court', reflects the opening words of such documents: *Sub
poena ...*, 'under penalty ...', which go on to specify that the
person summoned will be punished if the writ is not obeyed.

**sub quocunque titulo**
under whatever title

**sub rosa**
in strict confidence or secretly

In this age of covert operations, *sub rosa* is understood all too well and said all too often in English. The phrase is of interest primarily because it has the literal meaning 'under the rose'. The rose is a symbol of secrecy, perhaps deriving from a story involving Cupid, the Roman god of love, who is said to have given a rose to Harpocrates, the god of silence, as a bribe for not revealing the amorous activities of Venus, the goddess of sensual love, well known for practising what she preached. Roman dining-room ceilings were decorated with roses to remind guests not to make public things that might be said **sub vino** ('under the influence of wine').

**sub verbo**
under the word

A scholar's term, abbreviated s.v. – for example, *'s.v. sine prole'*, used for making a cross-reference to an entry in a dictionary, encyclopedia, index or other portion of text.

**sufficit**
it is sufficient

**sui generis**
one of a kind

This phrase means literally 'of its (or his or her or their) own kind'. One should take some care in applying *sui generis*, lest the phrase lose its value. Properly used, *sui generis* requires that the person, place or thing be of an entirely distinctive character.

**summa cum laude**
with highest praise

See *cum laude*.


**summa sedes non capit duos**
there's room for only one at the top

Literally 'The highest seat does not hold two'. And that's the story in all corporations.


**summum bonum**
the highest good


**summum ius** (or **jus**) **summa iniuria** (or **injuria**)
extreme law, extreme injustice

Lawmakers and judges beware: strict enforcement of a law sometimes results in great injustice.


**summum nec metuas diem nec optes**
neither fear nor wish for your last day

One of Martial's epigrams.


**sumptus censum ne superet**
live within your means

One of Martial's epigrams, literally 'Let not your spending exceed your income'. Good advice for all but modern governments. It is worthwhile to reflect on the word *censum* in this epigram. The Roman *census*, conducted every five years, registered all citizens in classes according to their property holdings. So *census* came to mean 'wealth' and 'property', and a poor Roman could be called **homo sine censu**, literally 'a man without property'.

**suo iure** (or **jure**)
in one's own right or in its own right

**suo motu**
spontaneously

Literally 'by one's own motion' or 'by its own motion'.

**suo tempore**
at one's own time or at its own time

**supra**
above

A scholar's word, used to make reference to an earlier portion of a text, usually in the phrase **vide supra**, 'See above'.

**supremum vale**
farewell for the last time

Before death, that is.

**sursum corda**
lift up your hearts

Heard in the Mass.

**sutor, ne supra crepidam**
cobbler, stick to your last

See *ne supra crepidam sutor iudicaret*.

**suum cuique pulchrum**
love is blind

Literally 'To everyone, his own is beautiful'. Alone, *suum cuique* may be rendered as 'to each his own'.

**s.v.**

Abbreviation of **sub verbo**, 'under the word'. A lexicographer or encyclopaedist's phrase, informing readers that the entry for a specified word or topic – for example, '*s.v. quorum*' – contains information germane to the subject under discussion to which reference is made.

# T

## tabula rasa
a clean slate

This phrase, literally 'a scraped writing tablet', is used most often to denote a mind devoid of preconceptions. Thus, a person who has practised hunt-and-peck typewriting for most of his adult life must become a *tabula rasa* before he can learn to use the touch system, and a newborn child is presumed to be a *tabula rasa*.

## tacent, satis laudant
silence is praise enough

A line from Terence's *Eunuchus*, literally 'They are silent, they praise enough', recognizing that rapt attention in an audience can be more flattering than applause.

## tacet
be silent

A musical notation, literally 'It is silent', directing a singer or instrumentalist to maintain silence during the portion of a score so marked.

## taedium vitae
ennui or *Weltschmerz*

Literally 'weariness of life'.

## tam facti quam animi
as much in deed as in intention

**tamquam alter idem**
as if a second self

See *alter idem*.


**tangere ulcus**
to touch a sore

This expression is used with the meaning of 'to hit the nail on the head' and with the meaning of 'to touch a sore spot'.


**tarde venientibus ossa**
for latecomers, the bones

See *sero venientibus ossa*.


**telum imbelle sine ictu**
an ineffectual argument

In Virgil's *Aeneid*, aged Priam throws a *telum imbelle sine ictu*, literally 'a feeble weapon without a thrust', giving us a metaphor for an argument that falls short of the mark or misses it altogether.


**tempora mutantur nos et mutamur in illis**
times change and we change with them

Attributed to John Owen, died 1622, a Welshman known for his Latin epigrams.


**tempori parendum**
one must keep abreast of the time

An essential thought – literally 'One must yield to time' – for anyone who wishes to remain in the swim. A related expression is **temporibus inserviendum**, literally 'One must pay attention to the times'.


**temporis ars medicina fere est**
time is a great healer

This phrase, literally 'Time usually is the best means of healing', may have application in the field of medicine, but it appears in

Ovid's *Remedia Amoris*, which is concerned with the amatory rather than the medical arts.

### tempus abire tibi est
make way for someone else

Horace, in his *Epistles*, giving all of us excellent advice. When we have ceased being productive, it is time to make room for those who are. Horace put it this way: 'You have played enough, eaten and drunk enough.' Now *tempus abire tibi est*, literally 'It is time for you to go away'. Senior faculty, superannuated executives, old soldiers and politicians, hearken unto Horace.

### tempus edax rerum
time, the devourer of all things

Ovid, in *Metamorphoses*, calling our attention to the irreversible results – both good and bad – of the passage of time.

### tempus fugit
time flies

Who doesn't know this?

### tempus ludendi
a time for playing

Workaholics, take heed. All work and no play ...

### tempus omnia revelat
time reveals all things

So wait.

### tenax propositi
resolute

Literally 'tenacious of purpose'.

**tenere lupum auribus**
to take the bull by the horns

This phrase, literally 'to hold a wolf by the ears', implies fearlessness in confronting a dangerous situation or boldness in dealing with a difficulty.

**te nosce**
know thyself

A Latin translation of a precept incised in the stone of the temple of the oracle at Delphi, reflecting the oracle's interest in individual morality.

**teres atque rotundus**
well-rounded

Horace's phrase, in the *Satires*, literally 'polished and round', describing the Stoics' conception of a wise man as one who rolls smoothly through life. The full phrase is **totus teres atque rotundus**, 'complete, polished and round'.

**terra es, terram ibis**
'dust thou art, to dust thou shalt return'

This entry comprises a well-known line from Genesis as rendered in Latin in the Vulgate and in English in the King James Version. The edition of the Bible known as the Vulgate, from the Latin **editio vulgata**, 'the common edition', first appeared in print in 1456, after translation more than a thousand years earlier by St Jerome. The King James Version, also known as the King James Bible (1611), was produced at the direction of King James VI and I (1567/1603–25) by a team of scholars who worked for several years, relying on existing English translations. The line *terra es, terram ibis* is the one in which God explains the consequences of Adam's disobedience. In one stanza of 'A Psalm of Life', Longfellow incorporated the King James translation of this melancholy line:

Life is real! Life is earnest!
And the grave is not its goal;
Dust thou art, to dust returnest,
Was not spoken of the soul.
(See *memento, homo, quia pulvis es et in pulverem revertis*.)


## terra firma
dry land

This well-known phrase literally means 'solid land'. It is used to differentiate land from sea.


## terra incognita
unknown territory

This phrase is used to designate a subject or place about which nothing or next to nothing is known. 'Modern physics, by its nature, continually concerns itself with *terra incognita*.'


## testis unus, testis nullus
one witness, no witness

A legal maxim indicating that unsupported testimony is no better than complete absence of testimony, and suggesting to all of us that we not give full credence to a story we hear from one source only.


## timeo Danaos et dona ferentes
when an enemy appears friendly, watch out

This advice, literally 'I fear the Greeks [ancient name Danai], even when bearing gifts', comes from Virgil's *Aeneid* and is addressed to the men of Troy. The Trojans were told by one of their priests to mistrust the huge wooden horse – the fabled Trojan horse – left behind by the departing soldiers of Greece, ostensibly as an offering to the gods to secure safe passage for Ulysses during his return to Greece. Ignoring the advice, the Trojans did not look the gifthorse in the mouth but dragged it inside their city, with predictable results. Recall that it contained a contingent of Greek soldiers sufficiently numerous to open the city gates and admit enough additional troops to destroy Troy. The irony is that Troy, not Greece, is stigmatized in the naming of the wooden horse. To this day, 'a Trojan horse' is a thing or person that subverts from within. The Greeks come in for their share of opprobrium in the expression 'Greek gifts', today scarcely cited, except as *timeo Danaos et dona ferentes* and its translation.

## timeo hominem unius libri
I fear the man of one book

An observation attributed to Aquinas, with two possible interpretations. The older, more customary interpretation has it that a person steeped in a single source is a formidable opponent in debate. In a more recent interpretation, *timeo hominem unius libri* expresses fear in confronting a man for whom the knowledge, opinions and dogma of a single book are sufficient and who recognizes no truths but the literal statements of his own book.

## toga
a toga

The toga is well known as the standard Roman outer garment. It was a white woollen upper garment worn in public by men in times of peace as a sign of their status as citizens. Freedmen and freedwomen also wore the toga, but women of higher status wore the **stola**, a long outer garment. The adjective *togata* was applied to women of doubtful reputation, an indication that the practice of judging a book by its cover, or a person by the way he or she dresses, did not originate in modern times.

## totidem verbis
in so many words

## totis viribus
with all one's powers

## toto caelo
diametrically opposite

We say the views of two people or two governments are 'worlds apart', but the Romans said they were separated *toto caelo*, literally 'by the entire heavens'.

**totus teres atque rotundus**
well-rounded

See *teres atque rotundus*.


**tu ne cede malis sed contra audentior ito**
yield not to misfortunes, but advance all the more boldly against them

Advice for all of us, from Virgil's *Aeneid*.


**tu quoque**
you too

A retort to an accusation. You are guilty of the very misdeeds or mistakes you attribute to me; it takes one to know one.

## ubi bene ibi patria
I owe my allegiance to the country in which I prosper

A patriotic Roman sentiment, also expressed as **ubi libertas** ('liberty') **ibi patria**, 'Where there is freedom, there is my fatherland'.

## ubi mel ibi apes
honey attracts bees

This saying from Plautus, literally 'Where there is honey, there will be bees', reminds us that there is a sure-fire way to attract followers.

## ubi solitudinem faciunt pacem appellant
they create desolation and call it peace

A more literal translation of this line from Tacitus's *Agricola* is 'Where they create a desert, they call it peace'. Tacitus was quoting the leader of the Britons, who had made the mistake of coming out second best in a war against the invading armies of the Romans. While the Romans customarily treated conquered peoples with respect, their destruction of Carthage and sack of Corinth were notable exceptions.

## ultima forsan
it's later than you think

These words, literally 'perhaps the last', are sometimes inscribed on the face of a clock to convey the thought that the moment of death – indeed, the moment of eternal judgement – may be at hand. The prudent person treats every hour as though it were his last.

**ultima ratio**
the final argument

This phrase has literal applications – for example, 'We find many reasons for denying your loan application, but your four bankruptcies are the *ultima ratio.*' Louis XIV of France, recognizing that force is the final argument, directed that his cannons carry the legend **ultima ratio regum** ('of kings'). As a result, *ultima ratio regum* signifies 'war'.

**ultima Thule**
the end of the world

Ancient mariners believed that the northern end of the world was an island called Thule, which stood six days' sail from Britain. The precise location of Thule is not known today, but *ultima Thule*, mentioned in Virgil's *Georgics*, survives as a useful expression for describing any place whose appearance gives one the feeling of standing at the end of the world.

**ultimum vale**
farewell for the last time

See *supremum vale.*

**ultra vires**
beyond legal authority

A court or other agency of government that exceeds its legal authority in a particular matter is said to be acting *ultra vires*, literally 'beyond the powers'.

**una salus victis nullam sperare salutem**
knowing there is no hope can give one the courage to fight and win

Virgil, in the *Aeneid*, gives us this insight, which translates more literally as 'The one safety for the vanquished is to abandon hope for safety'. Thus, when we know we are doomed, we take risks we would dismiss as imprudent if we thought we still had a chance. This is the stuff that brings dazed prizefighters back to their feet at a count of nine.

**una voce**
unanimously

Literally 'with one voice'.


**unguibus et rostro**
with all one's might

When the Romans fought *unguibus et rostro*, they fought 'with claws and beak'. After all, they used the eagle as their device on banners etc. We moderns are sometimes said to fight 'tooth and nail', which implies that we bite and scratch, and some of us have been known to claw our way to the top. Civilization marches on.


**unus vir nullus vir**
two heads are better than one

This Roman proverb translates literally as 'one man, no man', giving the sense shown above. But it can also be taken in a second sense: before machines came along, many heavy tasks were beyond the strength of a person working alone, so *unus vir nullus vir*, 'one man, no man'.


**urbi et orbi**
to the city and the world

In papal blessings and documents addressed *urbi et orbi*, the city is Rome, the world the rest of humanity.


**usque ad aras**
even to the altars

See *amicus usque ad aras*.


**usque ad nauseam**
even to the point of (inducing) nausea

See *ad nauseam*.

**usus promptos facit**
practice makes perfect

Literally 'Use makes men ready'. A related proverb is **usus te plura docebit**, 'Experience will teach you many things'. And then there is **usus est optimum magister**, 'Experience is the best teacher'.

**utcumque placuerit Deo**
howsoever it shall please God

**ut fata trahunt**
at the mercy of destiny

Literally 'as the fates drag'. This expression recognizes that we have limited control over our lives. 'We have done all we can; from here on, it's *ut fata trahunt.*'

**ut infra**
as cited below

A scholar's phrase, literally 'as below'. See *ut supra* and *vide*.

**uti non abuti**
treat with respect

Literally 'to use, not abuse'.

**uti possidetis**
we stole it fair and square

The principle, literally 'As you possess', that one is entitled to keep what one has acquired. It is applied most often during diplomatic negotiations prior to a peace treaty. According to *uti possidetis*, the territory a country has won during a war may be retained by that country from then on. The principle works well because strong countries usually win wars and can continue to work their will. It does not work well when a comparatively weak nation happens to win a war against an even weaker adversary. At that point, the great powers usually team up to arrange for return of conquered territory to the defeated nation. So *uti possidetis*, 'As you possess', depends on who the 'you' is.

**ut supra**
as cited above

A scholar's phrase, literally 'as above'. See *ut infra* and *vide*.

**vade in pace**
go in peace

A Roman way to say goodbye.

**vade mecum**
go with me

A *vade mecum* is usually a small manual or reference book that is regularly carried in one's pocket – today a *vade mecum* as often as not travels in a handbag or in the ubiquitous attaché case – because it contains information that is frequently consulted. A *vade mecum* may also be something other than a small book: a pocket calculator, a portable dictating machine, even a personal computer.

**vade retro me, Satana**
get thee behind me, Satan

The well-known phrase in Mark's Gospel in which Jesus rebukes Peter, concluding 'For thou mindest not the things of God, but the things of men'. (See *apage Satanas*.)

**vae soli**
woe to the solitary men

Bachelors, take heed.

**vae victis**
it's tough to be a loser

The words, literally 'woe to the vanquished', attributed by Livy to Brennus, a chief of the Gauls arranging terms of peace with the

Romans in 390 BC. According to Livy, when the Romans complained that the Gauls were using excessive weights in measuring the amount of gold the Romans were to pay, Brennus threw his sword onto the weights, exclaiming, '*Vae victis*'. Brennus was telling the Romans that he, not they, had the upper hand.

### vale
farewell

See *ave atque vale*.

### valeat quantum valere potest
take it for what it's worth

Literally "Let it stand for what it is worth." Appropriate when passing information of doubtful authenticity.

### valete ac plaudite
let's give them a hand!

The words, literally 'Farewell and applaud', said at the end of a Roman play. Remember that theatres were not equipped with curtains in those days. (See *plaudite, cives*.)

### vanitas vanitatum, omnis vanitas
everything man does is in vain

This phrase from Ecclesiastes is often given the literal translation 'Vanity of vanities, all is vanity', leading to a misunderstanding of what is intended. When it is understood that *vanitas* means 'emptiness' or 'fruitlessness', the true intention of Ecclesiastes is perceived.

### varia lectio
a variant reading

A scholar's phrase. The plural is **variae lectiones**.

### variorum
of various persons

The English word 'variorum', also given as 'variorum edition', is a shortened form of the Latin **cum notis variorum**, 'with the notes of various persons'. 'Variorum' has two applications in English. It is used to designate an edition or a text containing the notes of various scholars and to designate an edition supplying variant readings of a text. The full Latin phrase for a variorum or a variorum edition is **editio cum notis variorum**. Variorums generally supply both comments by various scholars and variant readings of a text.

### varium et mutabile semper femina
*la donna è mobile*

This is the argument, literally 'Woman is ever fickle and changeable', advanced to Aeneas as a sound reason for leaving Dido, and thanks to Virgil – and to Giuseppe Verdi's *Rigoletto* – it has been parroted ever since, perhaps primarily by men. Let the record – according to Virgil at least – show that lovelorn Dido committed suicide by fire after Aeneas departed. So who was fickle? On the other hand, if the story can be believed, it does appear that old flames die.

### vel caeco appareat
it's obvious

Literally 'It would be apparent even to a blind man'.

### velis et remis
an all-out effort

Literally 'with sails and oars', also given as **remis velisque**. What would the Romans have said if they had invented the jet aeroplane?

### veni, vidi, vici
I came, I saw, I conquered

The best-known Latin sentence of them all, freely rendered as 'a piece of cake', reported by Plutarch to have been uttered by Julius Caesar by way of reporting his victory in 47 BC over Pharnaces, King of Pontus.

**verbatim et litteratim**
accurately rendered

Literally 'word for word and letter for letter'. To this phrase is sometimes appended **et punctatim**, 'and point for point'.

**verba volant, scripta manent**
get it down on paper

Literally 'Spoken words fly away, written words remain'.

**verbum sat sapienti**
a word to the wise

Literally 'A word is enough for a wise man'.

**veritas odium parit**
truth breeds hatred

Terence, in *Andria*, telling us it is not always wise to be frank with one's friends.

**veritas simplex oratio est**
the language of truth is simple

By contrast, with apologies to Sir Walter Scott: 'Oh, what a tangled web we weave, When first we practise to deceive!'

**veritas vos liberabit**
the truth shall make you free

**verso**
left

This term is used to indicate a left-hand page of a book, the full Latin phrase being **verso folio**, literally 'the page being turned'. (See *recto*.)

**versus**
against

## via
a way

This word gives us several interesting combinations. **Via Appia**, 'the Appian Way', leads from Rome to Brindisi (ancient name **Brundisium**). **Via Dolorosa**, 'the road of sadness', is the road Jesus followed on the way to His crucifixion. **Via media**, 'the middle way', is the moderate course so frequently recommended in Latin proverbs. Another bit of Roman advice is **via trita, via tuta**, which translates as 'The beaten path is the safe path', *Via* has also given us an English preposition meaning 'by way of' or 'through'.

## vice versa
conversely

A phrase we all know in English. The Latin words translate literally as 'the change being turned'.

## victis honor
let's give the losers a hand!

Literally 'honour to the vanquished'.

## vide
see

*Vide* gives us several useful expressions. **Vide et crede**, 'See and believe'. **Vide infra**, 'See below', used by scholars to refer a reader to something that follows in a text. **Vide supra**, 'See above', a scholar's way of referring a reader to something that appears earlier in a text.

## videlicet
namely

Commonly abbreviated viz., which is expressed orally as 'namely', not as 'viz.' *Videlicet*, literally 'It is permitted to see', is also translated as 'to wit'.

**video meliora proboque, deteriora sequor**
even though I know better, I keep on doing the wrong thing

A line from Ovid's *Metamorphoses*, literally 'I see the better way and approve it, but I follow the worse way', confirming what we know too well about recidivism.

**vi et armis**
by force of arms

**vigilate et orate**
watch and pray

About all one can do in the nuclear age.

**vincam aut moriar**
I will conquer or die

**vincit qui patitur**
patience wins

Literally 'He prevails who is patient'.

**vincit qui se vincit**
first we must learn to overcome our own bad habits

This advice, literally 'He conquers who conquers himself', perhaps appropriate for display in a psychotherapist's office, recognizes that most of us have traits or habits that are less than desirable. By changing our ways, we make it possible to win out in larger arenas. *Vincit qui se vincit* is an adaptation of one of Syrus's maxims, **bis vincit qui se vincit in victoria**, which has a narrower meaning but one worth learning because it calls attention to the human tendency to gloat: 'He conquers twice who conquers himself in victory.'

**vincit veritas**
truth wins

Even though it may take a long time. This sanguine thought may also be expressed as **vincit omnia veritas**, 'Truth conquers all things'.

**vinculum matrimonii**
the bond of matrimony

*Vinculum* may also be translated as 'noose' or 'chain'.


**virginibus puerisque canto**
I chant to maidens and to boys

A line in Horace's *Odes*.


**viribus totis**
with all one's strength


**viribus unitis**
with forces united


**viri infelicis procul amici**
success has many friends

Those who achieve eminence or wealth find suddenly that they are surrounded by friends but when their fortunes have changed find just as suddenly that they are alone. *Viri infelicis procul amici*, literally 'Friends stay far away from an unfortunate man', affirms that fair-weather friends are friends we can rely on as along as we don't have to. (See *felicitas habet multos amicos*.)


**vir sapit qui pauca loquitur**
know when to hold your tongue

Literally 'That man is wise who talks little'. (See *cave quid dicis, quando, et cui* for another way of giving this same advice.)


**virtus post nummos**
keep your eye on the bottom line

This cynical advice – one man's cynicism is another man's wisdom – freely adapted from one of Horace's *Epistles*, translates literally as 'virtue after wealth'. The full thought is **quaerenda pecunia primum est virtus post nummos**, which may be translated as 'Money is to be sought after first of all, virtue after wealth'.

**virtus probata florescit**
grace under pressure

A maxim, literally 'Manly excellence flourishes in trial', suggesting that we learn our true character only when we put ourselves to the test and come out on top.

**virtute et armis**
by courage and arms

**virtutis fortuna comes**
good luck is the companion of courage

The suggestion is that good things don't just happen; we must prepare ourselves to grasp opportunity when it comes our way.

**vis consili expers mole ruit sua**
discretion is the better part of valour

An observation from one of Horace's *Odes*, literally 'Force without good sense falls by its own weight'.

**vis inertiae**
the power of inactivity

It is to *vis inertiae* that we ascribe the willingness of many people to put up with their troubles rather than change their lives and risk encountering new and possibly more vexing troubles. With *inertiae* translated as 'of inertia' *vis inertiae* explains why a plan set in motion is difficult to stop, and vice versa.

**vita brevis, ars longa**
life is short, art is long

See *ars longa, vita brevis*.

**vitam impendere vero**
to devote one's life to the truth

A noble resolve from Juvenal's *Satires*.

**vitam regit fortuna non sapientia**
it's mostly a matter of luck

Literally 'Chance, not wisdom, governs human life'.


**vita non est vivere sed valere vita est**
life is more than merely staying alive

One of Martial's epigrams, literally 'Life is not to live, but life is to be strong, vigorous'. Food for thought for all of us.


**vivamus, mea Lesbia, atque amemus**
let's live it up

Advice from Catullus, in one of his poems, literally 'Lesbia mine, let's live and love'. (See *carpe diem*.)


**vivat**
long live …

**Vivat regina**, 'Long live the queen'. **Vivat rex**, 'Long live the king'.


**viva voce**
orally

A *viva voce*, also a 'viva voce examination', is an oral examination. To respond *viva voce* is to respond orally, rather than in writing. The Latin phrase literally means 'with the living voice'.


**vive hodie**
live today

From one of Martial's epigrams, telling us in full that it is not wise to say 'I'll live tomorrow'; tomorrow is for tomorrow's living. *Vive hodie*. (See *carpe diem* for a fuller explanation.)

**vivere parvo**
to live on little

Little income, that is.


**vive ut vivas**
live that you may live

Sound advice on how to conduct one's life, albeit contrary to that given in *carpe diem*.


**vive, vale**
farewell

Literally 'Live, be well', also given as **vive valeque**, 'Live and be well'.


**vixere fortes ante Agamemnona**
we don't have a monopoly on all that is good

This line from Horace's *Odes* tells us literally that 'Brave men lived before Agamemnon'. The words that follow this line translate as 'all unwept and unknown, lost in the distant night, since they lack a divine poet'. Thus, Horace tells us that great acts of heroism, kindness and the like have often been performed by unsung heroes – unsung in the sense that no record was made of their exploits – yet even though we know nothing of those acts, we must not assume they never happened. The public relations industry flourishes because it understands that perception of events may count for more than the events themselves.


**vixit**
he or she has lived

A word found on tombstones, usually **vixit ... annos**, 'He or she lived (a certain number of) years'.

**viz.**
Abbreviation of *videlicet*.

**volens et potens**
willing and able

**volente Deo**
God willing

See *Deo volente*.

**volenti non fit iniuria** (or **injuria**)
to a willing person no wrong is done

The legal maxim we all know, for example, in the phrase 'consenting adults'.

**volo, non valeo**
I am willing but unable

**voluptates commendat rarior usus**
all pleasure's no pleasure

Juvenal, in his *Satires*, counselling moderation in living the good life. Literally 'Rare indulgence increases pleasures'.

**vox clamantis in deserto**
the voice of one crying in the wilderness

Familiar words from various books of the New Testament, in Matthew continuing 'Prepare you the way of the Lord; make his paths straight'.

**vox et praeterea nihil**
empty words

Plutarch's phrase, used to denote an empty threat. Plutarch tells a story of a man who plucks the feathers from a nightingale. Finding that its body *sans* plumage is pathetically small, he remarks, '*Vox et praeterea nihil*, 'Literally 'A voice and nothing more'.

**vox populi vox Dei**
the voice of the people is the voice of God

Political leaders take heed: the wishes of the people are irresistible.

**vulneratus non victus**
bloodied but unbowed

Literally 'wounded but not conquered'.

**vultus est index animi**
the face is the mirror of the soul

Literally 'The expression on one's face is a sign of the soul'.

# English Index